THE JOB OF A LAUGHTIME

The Complete Comedy Writer

Nine simple lessons on creating your own comedy
from gags to sitcoms.

First published in 2011

By Lulu.com

email: ashtons@london.com

ISBN 978-1-4710-2129-9

Printed and bound by Lulu.com

THE JOB OF A LAUGHTIME

BY BRAD ASHTON

BRAD ASHTON'S COMEDY WRITING COURSE - NINE LESSONS

This lesson shows how simple it is to create gags. We examine the many formulae and suggest a variety of every-day subjects to apply those formulae to for guaranteed laughs.

In Lesson Two we see how comedy routines are made up by stringing together the gags we have created on any chosen subject so that each gag appears to lead in to the next. It also deals with the different distinctive styles of stand-up comedians.

Black-outs usually last about ten seconds, Quickies are up to a minute and modern sketches no longer than two and a half minutes. There are a myriad forms of sketches and in this lesson we deal with writing the most saleable.

Comedy journalism is a well paid market because it's specialised and too few writers attempt it. In effect, it's much easier than you might think. It mostly involves looking at an ordinary subject in an extraordinary way. In this lesson you'll be taken through the thought process and given examples of the results.

LESSON FIVE - Characters And Their Relationships In Situation Comedies.

This will be our first dip into the world of situation comedy that all new writers aspire to. Here we see how new characters are drawn from closely observing the people around us. Then we surround those characters with other contrasting people with whom they make contact and will highlight their differences.

LESSON SIX - Formulating Ideas For A Sitcom Series

These ideas often come from personal experiences that, with a little exaggeration or adjustment can provide the basis for your long-running series. If you are a doctor, lawyer, accountant, estate agent, tax inspector or whatever, you'll have inside knowledge of the comic side of your profession or trade. This lesson shows how some of TV's most popular formats started from the germ of an idea.

LESSON SEVEN - Writing Sitcom Dialogue

Dialogue in sitcoms is not just for getting laughs (though that is, of course essential), it must reveal the characteristics of the person delivering it. It also has to advance the storyline. This lesson shows how writers ensure laughs without deviating from the plot.

LESSON EIGHT - The Complete Situation Comedy Script.

By now you will have mastered the art of writing your very own sitcom script. Here is an example of what the finished product will look like.

LESSON NINE - Selling Your Work

Whether you have written gags, routines, sketches, magazine articles or situation comedies you need to know how to go about selling them. This final lesson covers that with names and addresses you'll find very useful.

PREFACE

Do you ever wake up in the morning feeling you want to do some crazy things, like phoning the maternity hospital and asking if they deliver; or buying a roasting turkey and taking it to a taxidermist to be stuffed; or taking up a collection to buy toupees for bald eagles? If you do, you have the makings of a good comedy writer.

You will be the kind of person asking rhetorical questions like has Old McDonald ever been cautioned for keeping a noisy farm? Is it a plastic surgeon's job to pick your nose for you? Would you expect something in mint condition to have a hole in it? Are Sunday drivers actually Friday drivers still looking for a place to park? Is a rare coin something you have left over after paying your taxes?

You'll begin to wonder whether Jewish kids have piggy banks: Snow White had an eighth dwarf who was gay and named "Sweetie": or when policeman arrests a mime artist, does he tell him he has the right to remain silent?

In your mind's eye you'll see crazy things like a football ground's AstroTurf sprouting plastic weeds. A circus's two-headed lady on her wedding night claiming that both have headaches. A woman being kicked out of a nudist camp for putting dressing on her salad.

You'll imagine crazy door signs like those outside a dentist PRESS BELL THEN OPEN WIDE… a police station WE'RE CLOSED BUT LEAVE YOUR NAME AND FINGERPRINTS… Weight Watchers GONE TO LUNCH, BACK IN 150 CALORIES… Santa's Grotto TWO KNEES – NO WAITING… Sado-masochist's parlour HOUSE OF WHACKS… Quarantine hospital THE BUG STOPS HERE… An Abbey NUN SMOKING AREA… an aviary HOME TWEET HOME.

English is a very rich language which readily lends itself to gags and jokes. It may be hard for you to imagine right now, but once you've read through this book you'll be convinced that you can always replace a frown with a smile.

Comedy has its rules, customs and formulae. Once you have learnt those you have millions of subjects to apply them to with the guarantee of raising a smile, a titter or a guffaw.

Doctors tell us laughter is the best medicine. But you won't need seven years at medical school to qualify as a dispenser of that medicine. Anyone can create laughter. It's not a gift or talent you have to be born with. It can be taught. And that's what this book sets out to prove.

If you need more motivation, let me tell you of some of the perks I have enjoyed as a comedy writer, besides the high payments of course. As a comedy writer you'll get to meet and work with top TV, radio and stage stars and travel at someone else's expense to attend meetings, conferences and rehearsals in countries around the world. You (and your friends, relatives and neighbours) see your name on the credits of top TV shows. You'll be invited to give paid talks to groups such as The Rotarians, Round Tables, Women's Institutes, Townswomen's Guilds and U3As. And there are dozens of comedy writers (including myself), who regularly get free cruises for just regaling other passengers with backstage stories of the shows and stars we've been associated with in our work. I have enjoyed all of those perks, including sixty cruises so far, and you can too.

But even if you've no inclination to be a humorous scribe, creating comedy provides other wonderful benefits. Most women, for instance, will tell you that the thing they found most attractive in a man was his sense of humour. "He made me laugh a lot."

Many of us have been prevailed upon to "Say a few words…" at a family or social gathering. If you can make those few words funny you will be remembered and head the ever-popular guest list.

Every salesman will tell that humour breaks down barriers and establishes a friendly rapport with their prospective customers. This book will help them continually re-stock their collection of funny stories.

Comedy is even appropriate at funerals. I remember attending Jimmy Jewel's cremation where fellow comedian Alfred Marks' eulogy included "I spent six months co-starring with Jimmy in *The Sunshine Boys*. He was such a hypochondriac that he even put in his will that he had to be buried next to a doctor." It got a huge laugh and helped make a mournful occasion into a merry one.

I am frequently asked what I think of the modern day stand-up comedians. My usual retort is that I try *not* to think of them. Too many rely on gags and routines about subjects that used to be banned on television and I think still ought to be. Humour based on drugs, overt sex and other bodily functions have their rightful place in nightclubs and stag do's where the audience expect that sort of thing. But when it's served up on TV it usually scores low in the ratings because it is too embarrassing for families to watch together. I have therefore, in this book, tended to veer away from that vein of humour and concentrate solely on the kind of comedy which I think is much more acceptable to a mass audience and can be written and performed without offence.

I loved writing this book and passing on the lessons I've learned over half a century of keeping comedians from being speechless.

BRAD ASHTON

LESSON ONE – The Art of Creating Gags

When I started out as a budding comedy writer there were no schools or correspondence courses that covered this subject. I learnt about creating comedy while serving my two years as a National Serviceman in the R.A.F. During the day I ran the Operations Room at Hendon Aerodrome and spent the evenings listening to every comedy programme available on radio at that time. They included the top American shows which were broadcast on short wave to the troops stationed in Germany.

Humour is contagious, if you hear a good joke you can't wait to pass it on. My memory has never been good, so I wrote down every gag, sketch idea and sitcom plot in order to relate them later to my airmen colleagues. Altogether I filled up six complete notebooks, which I still have in my attic.

It probably took about six months before it dawned on me that the material was becoming familiar. The same gag forms, sketch ideas and sitcom storylines were being used on most of the shows. Though the writers disguised them by changing the characters, locales and wording, I finally realised they were using the same formulae to get their laughs. Yes, comedy writing is done by formula. Teaching you those formulae is what this course is all about.

Way back in the 18th century a man named Joe Miller was credited with saying there were only seven jokes. He actually meant joke formulae. It may well have been true that there were only seven in those days, but now there are many, many more. Bob Hope claimed to have 7,000,000 gags in his files. Bob Monkhouse once told me he had 4,000,000 and was adding new ones every day.

Hope had seven writers under permanent contract. Bob Monkhouse had four, of which, for a while, I was one. With TV appearances eating up so much material comedians need a constant supply of new gags to keep them on top. Lots of gag writers earn a handsome living supplying just gags. So-called improvisational shows such as *Have I Got News For You, Mock The Week* and *Never Mind The Buzzcocks* employ a team of writers backstage supplying the funny "ad libs".

Gags are the A-B-C of comedy. Whether you're writing a sitcom, sketch, comedy routine or even a humorous piece for a magazine you'll need to know how to fashion the words to get laughs. Gag writing is your starting point. As this lesson will show, it really isn't all that difficult.

Before we actually get down to work, let me tell you that, if you intend writing for any particular comedians, you should be sure what style of comedy they use. There are so many different types. For instance there are the **OBSERVATIONAL COMEDIANS** like Michael McIntyre and Peter Kay who talk about things we can identify with. **TOPICAL COMEDIANS** like Punt & Dennis base their gags on recent news items. **PROP COMEDIANS** such as Joe Pasquale do magic and visual gags with strange props in a similar style to Tommy Cooper, while Jack Dee is a **CYNICAL COMEDIAN** who sees the downside of everything. **GIMMICK COMEDIANS** Omid Djalalli and Felix Dexter joke about their ethnic origins. **STUPID COMEDIANS** like Jimmy Cricket get laughs by showing their ignorance. And, of course, you have the diminutive Ronnie Corbett and overweight Jo Brand who exploit their physical peculiarities to amuse us. Let's not forget too the **IMPRESSIONISTS**, including Rory Bremner and Alistair McGowan, who use all these forms when doing their impersonations.

We shall deal later in this course with writing gags tailored to individual comedians. But first we'll cover the mechanism a professional comedy writer employs to create gags. With practice, inventing gags will become a matter of routine. All you have to do is think like a comedy writer. I'll show you the best way to do just that.

Creating gags is really just a matter of elimination. Here's the simplest method:

First choose a subject or theme that you're quite familiar with. It should also be one that your prospective audience is *au fait* with. It's no use doing jokes about the Queen's corgis for a foreign audience. Or gags about lesser known politicians, or local customs or landmarks. For this particular lesson I'll choose MARRIAGE as our subject and examine its potential for gag fodder.

Now we have a subject, so we make a list of everything we can think of connected with that subject. It does not have to be in any order, though it might make it easier if we think of it chronologically. Here's what our list might look like. The courtship. The proposal. The wedding plans. The wedding ring. The church banns. The vicar. The bride. The groom. The wedding cake. The Best Man. The speeches. The wedding car. The flowers. The marriage certificate. Carrying over the threshold. Nuptial agreement. Sexual relations. The arguments. The in-laws. The domestic chores. Wife's cooking. The anniversary.

You can probably think of many more, but we have enough to start with. Now let's mull over each one and see if they offer enough scope for a gag. Courtship is the period during which the couple get to know each other. They're on their best behaviour and often change after they're wed.

If I wanted to be insulting I could say, "During our courtship my wife played hard to get. Now we're married, she's hard to take." or "Before we got wed I asked my wife to make love. She said 'Over my dead body!' Then we got married and I realised she wasn't kidding."

Most men find they have to pluck up courage before popping the question.

"I was full of spirit the day I proposed. Johnny Walker, I think it was." or "I would have gone down on one knee, but Valerie thought I was short enough already."

With the divorce rate being so high, it's considered sensible to make a pre-nuptial agreement.

"I wanted a pre-marital agreement. Just like the one Henry VIII had with Anne Boleyn." or "Our agreement was that after divorce we shared the house. And we did. She got the inside and I got the outside."

The wedding ring is a sign of commitment and the more expensive it is, the happier the bride.

"He wanted a ring she could wear for eternity, because that's how long it took him to pay for it." or "I asked the jeweller if he had any cheaper rings. He said 'Yes, sir, but they're holding up the curtains.' "

The wedding dress is white to symbolise purity and the bride likes it kept secret ahead of the big day.

"She insisted the wedding dress be kept secret. She even made the seamstress wear a blindfold." or "She was so pleased with the way the dress turned out, she ordered two."

Wedding ceremonies have been held in some pretty strange places. Many brides are worried about whether they're making a big mistake.

"Did you hear about the couple that got wed in a disused lavatory? It was a marriage of convenience." or "I remember our wedding ceremony well. I had trouble getting the ring on, because she wouldn't uncross her fingers."

It's during the first night the groom finds out if his bride is shy or perhaps even frigid.

"It wasn't till our wedding night I realised my wife was bi-sexual. Every time I mentioned sex, she said 'Bye!' " or "My wife even claims to have a headache going through the bed section at D.F.S."

It's standard practice for the tiered wedding cake to have miniature figures of the bride and groom on top.

"I knew I was in trouble when the figures on the cake were my wife and her mother." or "The cake had so much icing I thought the couple on top were going to be Torvill and Dean."

Couples that can afford it go to some romantic place abroad for their honeymoon and during that time they can hardly keep their hands off each other.

"For our honeymoon we spent a week in Paris. Mind you, it was Valerie did most of the spending." or "There was a honeymoon couple making love on the plane. The groom took exception when the stewardess asked him to put his bride back in the upright position."

It's an old tradition for the groom to carry his bride over the threshold into the new home. But it's not always easy.

"Liz Taylor's last husband never worked again after their wedding. She was so fat, he did his back in carrying her over the threshold." or "When Twiggy got married she was so thin her husband didn't bother carrying her over the threshold. He just slid her in through the letter box."

As I've said before, gag writers work on formulae. New ones are being invented all the time. Here are a few tried and true formulae that you can use over and over again without your audience recognizing they are laughing at the same thing in a different guise.

The PERSONALISED gag form.

Let's say you wanted to concoct gags about well known personalities. I'll list a few to get you started. The ground is already laid for you because the audience know their names and public's perception. In other words, what immediately springs to the mind when their names are mentioned?

Dolly Parton has a big bust.

"Singer Dolly Parton didn't find her feet till she was forty. Then someone loaned her a periscope."

Prince Charles has big ears.

"Prince Charles took Camilla to visit the elephants at London Zoo. He wanted to show her someone with bigger ears than he has."

Bruce Forsyth is old, but still performing.

"No one knows how old Bruce Forsyth is. They are still carbon dating his birth certificate."

Liz Taylor was quite fat.

"Liz Taylor was so overweight she didn't just cast a shadow, she caused an eclipse."

Paul McCartney paid his second wife a fortune when they got divorced.

"They asked Paul McCartney how his second wife took it when they got divorced. He said 'In cash!' "

Now that you have the general idea, look at these celebrities and see if you can figure out what the punch lines to the next five gags might be. The answers are at the end of this lesson, but don't peek until you've spent some time working on them:

Ex President Bill Clinton has an eye for the ladies.

Jonathan Ross was paid a huge salary by the BBC.

Delia Smith presents cooking programmes on television.

Clint Eastwood's got a famous catchphrase.

Twiggy has a beanpole figure.

If you run these facts through your mind, you'll see how easy they are to target them for gags. Here are the gags for you to complete:

1. "When Clinton stayed at The Ritz in London he put in a call for seven. So they...."

2. "They say talk is cheap. That can't be true. Jonathan Ross got...."

3. "TV cook Delia Smith's just made out her will. It says she has to be...."

4. "Clint Eastwood's got a new girlfriend. He makes...."

5. "I'm told Twiggy had breast implants. If it's true, they must have...."

The ASSUMPTION gag.

In this form the audience is misled into assuming the comedian is talking about one thing, but they are surprised and amused when it turns out to be something different. The thoughts behind these gags were that:

A one man show usually means that there is just one performer. "Last night at a nightclub I did a one man show. Tonight I hope to have a bigger audience."

To a golfer the eighteenth is a hole not a calendar date. "When he told her he wanted them to marry on the 18th she didn't realize he meant on the golf course."

Not all starving people have no access to food. "Around the world there are millions of people starving. And that's just at Weight Watchers' meetings."

1948 can be something else besides a year. "I met her in 1948. That was her room number."

People expect the word "painter" to be associated with works of art. "He divorced his wife because he caught her posing naked for a painter. He wouldn't have minded, but this was a house painter."

Here are set-ups up of some assumption gags. Try figuring out how they finish.

1. "My wife and I are getting closer every day…. "
2. "For her birthday he gave her a bottle of toilet water from…."
3. "My wife finds it easy to tell a lie. She can tell it…."
4. "He knew she wanted something to wear on her finger. So he…."
5. "I bought a book called "The Best Way To Pick Up Girls". It turned out to be…."

The EXAGGERATION gag

Perhaps the most frequently used gag form is exaggeration when the comedian extends something to the point where it becomes ridiculous and funny.

These examples are self-explanatory and you don't need me to tell you how they were thought up.

"I ate a hamburger at one of those fast food restaurants. The meat was so thin I could have had three and still be a vegetarian."

"Those pizza places are now making the crusts so thin they can fax them to you."

"Liz Taylor put on so much weight. Last time she went to the opera no one would leave till she sang."

"Rubens used to paint overweight nudes. In fact, one was so fat instead of a paintbrush he used a roller."

"Everything at IKEA needs assembling. I bought a pillow there and they gave me a duck."

Test yourself by adding the appropriate endings.

1. "So many drugs are sold in that Disco, you have to have…"
2. "She has such a big mouth it takes her two hours to…."
3. "The aeroplane was so old it had…."
4. "He's such a great plumber, he could probably fix…."
5. "Those Smart cars are so small, one went into the back of me and…."

ILLOGICAL LOGIC

In this form something decidedly odd becomes acceptable in comedy.

"I told my wife I wanted a hot breakfast, so she set fire to my cornflakes."

"My brother spent £100 on a ticket to *Swan Lake* and complained because he couldn't hear a word."

"My doctor promised that jogging would add years to my life, and he was right. I already feel ten years older."

"The doctor told my wife to stop putting sugar in her coffee. So now she puts it straight in her mouth."

"My wife's just bought herself two sets of weighing scales. She always insists on a second opinion."

Add the ending you think would make these lines funny:

1. "They had trouble casting actors for *Twelve Angry Men*. All they could get were 10 angry men...."

2. "She wanted a man for all seasons, so she...."

3. "The recipe said 'separate two eggs'. So she...."

4. "The passport application form asked the question 'Length of residence in the U.K.?' She put down...."

5. "They say there's a £100 fine if you don't fill out the census form. But if you don't fill it out, how...."

IMPLIED gags

When a comedy writer wants to make a point without saying it, he uses the IMPLIED form of gag. This was Bob Hope's favourite form because it credited the audience with enough intelligence to recognize the point being subtly implied. Here are the messages behind these next few gags:

Kids are always tapping their parents for money. "Money isn't everything, but it's a good way of keeping in touch with your kids"

The comedian's wife is a less than competent cook. "In our house we didn't need a gong to tell us when dinner was ready. We had a smoke alarm."

During this recession most of us are winding up in debt. "The best selling commodity in Britain today is red ink."

Plumbers overcharge and end up wealthy. "I knew I wanted to be a plumber the moment I laid eyes on his Rolls Royce."

Some Cabinet Ministers aren't as clever as we'd like them to be. "Our Prime Minister keeps fit by exercising every day with his two dumbbells. The Chancellor of the Exchequer and the Foreign Secretary."

Can you complete these gags?

1. "There's no need to go to Disney in Paris, we have our own...."

2. "The flat-chested woman made a wish for two big boobs. She got...."

3. "The CIA bought every Des O'Connor record. They play them regularly in...."

4. "I'm finding household expenses even harder to keep down than...."

5. "I had to wait my turn at the hospital because the chap ahead of me had been shot in..."

INSULT

Sarcasm and denigrating remarks come under the umbrella heading of the INSULT gag. Providing there's no malice intended the audience will laugh along with you.

"I'm not saying that woman's fat, but Weight Watchers makes her pay double."

"She says she's just turned forty. It must have been a U-turn."

"Anne Robinson gets an allowance of £150,000 a year. And that's just for her make-up."

"Joan Collins has found the secret of eternal youth. She lies about her age.'

"This man has absolutely no respect for old age. Unless, of course, it comes out of a bottle."

Some further insults you ought to be able to work out.

1. "They say absence makes the heart grow fonder. That's true. The further my mother-in-law's...."

2. "That starlet's so vain. About the only time she isn't looking in a mirror is...."

3. "When you think of this man what immediately comes to mind is talent, good looks, charm and...."

4. "That woman's so full of wind they're...."

5. "Bruce Forsyth is known as the king of the one liners. That's because...."

LITERAL gags

The literal gag is where you use a well known saying in its literal meaning.

Here are a few recognisable phrases:

- Everyone loves a lover.

- One man, one vote.

- Service with a smile.

- Last night I had a heavy date.

- Two can live as cheaply as one.

Interpreted from a comedy writer's point of view there are literally hundreds of every-day expressions, proverbs, mottos and slogans with the potential to be the basis of a gag.

"Everyone loves a lover, except if it's your wife's lover."

"One man one vote. In some countries the dictator is the one man allowed to vote."

"You used to get service with a smile. Now if you expect service, they laugh."

"Last night I had a heavy date. She weighed sixteen stone."

"They say two can live as cheaply as one. But only if he's a schizophrenic."

See if your imagination can provide you with the cap to these lines.

1. "Their eyes met across a crowded room. It was…."

2. "This fellow got sacked for rubbing people up the wrong way. He was…."

3. "Whoever said figures don't lie never considered …."

4. "It's true that men don't cry. Except when they…."

5. "The way to a man's heart is through his stomach. That was first said by…."

The MALAPROPISM

American comedian Norm Crosby, the late Hylda Baker and Arthur Lucan of Lucan & McShane got their biggest laughs butchering the English language. That form of gag is called the MALAPROPISM. Here are a few examples alongside the words they were supposed to have said.

A manic depressive would be referred to as a "panic depressive."

Instead of opening a flat pack to read the instructions, it would be to read "the destructions."

A blood transfusion would be "blood confusion".

Sequence dancing would be "Sequins dancing."

Troilus and Cressida would become "Toilets and Cressida."

See if you can work out what or who is being referred to when the following Malapropisms are used.

1. David Cummerbund ….

2. Bruce Foreskin....

3. That holiday place, the Seashells....

4. Or the other place where they all speak French, Malicious....

5. That song from *Hair*, The Age Of Aquarium....

MENTAL PICTURES

Some gags present a funny mental picture in the mind of the listener which helps get the laugh. Here are a few:

"It's a case of reflected glory" as the Scotsman said when he walked over a moonlit puddle.

"After a woman reaches her peak, her other two peaks start to droop."

"I didn't realize how bad the crime in New York is till I went there and saw the Statue of Liberty had both hands up."

"Did you hear about the one-fingered pickpocket who could only steal polo mints?"

"Those Smart cars are so small, when out driving I put my hand out to turn right and one ran up my sleeve."

Can you provide the thoughts that complete these lines to make a mental picture?

1. "Certain people should avoid doing certain things. Like Dolly Parton...."

2. "The economy is going up and down like ...."

3. "Clinton never brought the country to its knees, except perhaps...."

4. "The good thing about those tiny Smart cars is you don't need a parking space. You just...."

5. He put on clean underwear every day. By the end of the week he...."

POLITICAL gags

The political gag is usually one that is sniping at the establishment and the people that run it. Today almost any gag that pokes fun at our political leaders will earn a loud laugh. They are the easiest of all targets because it seems none of us is ever completely satisfied with the way our country is run.

Let's set up the targets and see how many bulls eyes these score.

"The government has found a good way to reduce our electric bills. By keeping us in the dark."

"The Prime Minister has arthritic hands which is quite a handicap. Every time he makes a promise it takes him half an hour to uncross his fingers."

"The Prime Minister has the knack of making a long story short. He leaves out the facts."

"MPs look forward to their holiday breaks so they can spend time with their loved ones before going home to their wives."

"Some MPs have been using government money to get their lawns mowed, their moats cleared, their carpets laid and their lights fixed. We shouldn't complain. After all, they've got more people working than the last government ever did."

Using similar targets, see what you can make of these.

1. "I heard of an MP that was burgled three times. Once for...."

2. "George Bush was said to have told his secretary 'If there's any trouble anywhere in the world, I want to be woken up immediately. Even if...."

3. "Lots of good things have been said about Gordon Brown. I know, because ...."

4. "Gordon Brown can be credited with creating 2 million new jobs. Mostly in..."

5. "Ex-President Bill Clinton admits he had several love affairs, but insists his life's an open book, which...."

PUNS

Over the years puns have "groan" in popularity. They date back to Henry VIII's court jester where a *Newsnight* joke about Jeremy Axeman would have got him the chop. Some say that the main objection people have to puns is they didn't think of them first:

"A woman who taught her pet bird swear words was arrested for contributing to the delinquency of a Mynah."

"An Indian streaker was arrested and charged under the Obscene Public Asians Act."

"Ronnie Corbett was spotted asking directions to the Small Claims Court."

"Doctors put a postman in quarantine because they found out he was a carrier."

"My butcher refused to accept a bet that he couldn't reach the meat off the top shelf because he said the stakes were too high."

Can you identify these puns?

1. "Even riding stables are saying their customers...."
2. "For Christmas my wife bought me a smoking jacket. Took me...."
3. "The man who insisted on being cremated was just...."
4. "My plumber said last year business was flush, but now it's...."
5. "The lovebird left his mate because...."

RIDDLE or CONUNDRUM

A riddle or conundrum in comedy parlance is a question followed by an unexpected, usually silly, answer.

"What do you call a man who uses a faulty condom? Answer: Daddy!"

"How do you keep an idiot in suspense? Answer: I'll tell, you tomorrow."

"Why do actors tell each other to break a leg? Answer: It's the only sure way to get into a cast."

"What did the Hollywood starlet get that guaranteed her a part in a film? Answer: Undressed."

"What do you call an honest man in The House Of Commons? Answer: A visitor."

Following the same formula, try working out what the answer to these might be.

1. "Name five things that contain milk? Answer: Cheese, butter and…."

2. "Why are some people great fans of Red China? Answer: It looks lovely…."

3. "Why did the widow bury her tyrannical husband twelve feet under? Answer: Because deep down…."

4. "Before a farmer starts milking, what does he have to do? Answer: Make sure…."

5. "According to statistics, what's the longest a couple have ever been engaged? Answer: Depends on…."

RHETORICAL QUESTION

The rhetorical question is a similar form to the Riddle, but does not require an answer. It should be funny in itself. For instance:

"Does the name Quasimodo ring a bell?"

"Is someone who works the lights in a disco a quick flasher?"

"Does a belly dancer do navel manoeuvres?"

"How can a country with over a million divorces every year call itself the United States?"

"Do felines have cat scans?"

We'll assume that the audience know Quasimodo, the Hunchback Of Notre Dame, was a bell ringer. That lights in a Disco are meant to keep flashing. That belly dancers wiggle the area around their navels. That divorce breaks up the union of a married couple. And that a cat scan is a medical term in common usage.

See how well you fare in fitting endings to these lines?

1. "Will they ever stamp out …."
2. "If all the world's a stage, where are…."
3. "Why do they bother putting four wheels on supermarket trolleys when…."
4. "Was the man who trained his male rabbit to service 25 females a day just trying to…."
5. "Did the man who paid too much for his Sushi get…."

The VERNACULAR gag

This form allows the writer to choose a topic and refer to it in its own terms. The thought behind these next gags was that ghosts are also known as ghouls, librarians must register all books out on loan, many popular TV programmes are forever being repeated, butchers have names for sections of meat and brothels have a woman in charge. With these thoughts in mind, these gags should be self evident.

"As one ghost said to the other 'Thank heavens for little ghouls.' "

"When a librarian was admitted to hospital for surgery her colleagues sent her a Get Well card which read 'If they take anything out, make sure they sign for it.' "

"This week the founder of TV Times died. The funeral's at 10.00 a.m. with repeats tomorrow afternoon and Friday evening."

"The butcher told the doctor 'I've sprained something right here in the sirloin.' "

"The call girl told her husband ' I'm going home to Madam.' "

Following the clues in these straight lines, add the wording that completes the gag.

1. "A dentist married a manicurist. They've been fighting...."
2. "A salesman working on commission told his barber to...."
3. "Old Ma Kettle had four kids. Two with...."
4. "So many petrol garages are closing it's getting to be impossible to...."
5. "Twiggy's considering having a boob job because she wants to...."

Comedian Jack Benny always made himself the butt of his jokes. He said the best person to victimize in comedy is yourself. That way, no one is offended. That neatly leads me into...

The SELF DEPRECATION gag form.

Joan Rivers, the comedienne with a tongue sharp enough to slice a pineapple, says her philosophy is to make fun of herself first then her audience will more readily accept her gags against others. Here are examples of self deprecation gags.

"I'm often mistaken for Brad Pitt. When I tell people I look like Brad Pitt they say I'm mistaken."

"I left my girlfriend after five years because I couldn't stand her vulgar laughter. I hadn't noticed it till the day I proposed."

"I've been told I've got the perfect face for a comedian, especially for radio."

"I haven't seen my wife so happy since someone told her our marriage licence was expiring."

"I'm such a jinx, if one day I found myself on cloud nine, cloud ten would rain down on me."

Now it's your turn.

1. "My wife says she made a mistake when we got married. She says she should have…."

2. "My wife says I remind her of a whisky bottle. She says we're both ….."

3. "You too can have a body like mine, unless…."

4. "I performed my act to a room full of sick people. Mind you, they…."

5. "They say my act appeals mostly to the 18 to 30 group. That's not their age, it's…."

There are many other forms of gags and some of the gags I'm giving you are inter-changeable. But I'm sure you now have an insight into how a comedy writer uses contrasts, comparisons, word-plays and misconceptions to create his gags.

PERENNIALS

I have just one more point to make before ending this first lesson. It's about a form I haven't yet mentioned, PERENNIALS. These are gags that can be revived every time something happens that makes them once more appropriate. All you need to do is change the people or organisations:

"In a recent by-election the British National Party got 32 votes and demanded a recount. They couldn't believe they got that many."

"This year Royal Mail actually made a profit. It's being blamed on human error."

"At a Russell Brand show the producer was forced to employ twenty five security guards……to prevent the audience escaping."

"When overweight Jo Brand put on a bikini it was more revealing than the Chilcot Enquiry."

"The Prime Minister attends three different committee meetings a day. He's busier than two Sultans at a wife swapping party."

COMPLETED GAGS.

PERSONALISED.

1. "When Clinton stayed at The Ritz in London he put in a call for seven. So they sent up four blondes, two brunettes and a redhead."
2. "They say talk is cheap. That can't be true. Jonathan Ross got six million a year for it."
3. "TV cook Delia Smith's just made out her will. It says she has to be cremated in an oven at 350 degrees and left there until she's a golden brown."
4. "Clint Eastwood's got a new girlfriend. He makes her day and she makes his nights."
5. "I'm told Twiggy had breast implants. If it's true they must have put them in backwards."

ASSUMPTION

1. "My wife and I are getting closer every day, to killing each other."
2. "For her birthday he gave her a bottle of toilet water. From his own toilet."
3. "My wife finds it easy to tell a lie. She can tell it the moment I open my mouth."
4. "He knew she wanted something to wear on her finger, so he bought her an Elastoplast."
5. "I bought a book called *The Best Way To Pick Up Girls*. It turned out to be an instruction manual for ballet dancers."

EXAGGERATION

1. "So many drugs are sold in that disco; you have to have a prescription to get in."
2. "She has such a big mouth it takes her two hours to put on her lipstick."
3. "The aeroplane was so old it had an outside toilet."
4. "He's such a great plumber; he could probably fix the Niagara Falls."

5. "Those Smart cars are so small, one went into the back of me and it took the doctors four hours to remove it."

ILLOGICAL LOGIC

1. "They had trouble casting actors for *Twelve Angry Men*. All they could get were ten men that were angry and two who were very upset."
2. "She wanted a man for all seasons, so she married four different men."
3. "The recipe said 'separate two eggs', so she put one in the kitchen and one in the garage."
4. "The passport application form asked the question 'Length of UK residence?' She put down 'Thirty feet, not counting the garage.' "
5. "They say there's a £100 fine if you don't fill out the customs form. But if you don't fill it out, how can they find you?"

IMPLIED

1. "There's no need to go to Disney in Paris, we have our own Fantasy Land right here. It's called the Houses of Parliament."
2. "The flat-chested woman made a wish for two big boobs. She got Ken Livingstone and Alastair Darling."
3. "The CIA bought every Des O'Connor record. They play them regularly in Guantanamo Bay to torture the prisoners."
4. "I'm finding household expenses harder to keep down than airline food."
5. "I had to wait my turn at the hospital because the chap ahead of me had been shot in the Spanish Civil War."

INSULTS

1. "They say absence makes the heart grow fonder. That's true. The further my mother-in-law's away from me the more I like her."

2. "That starlet's so vain, the only time she isn't looking in a mirror is when she's parking the car."
3. "When you think of this man what immediately comes to mind is talent, good looks, charm and all those other things he doesn't have."
4. "That woman's so full of wind they're naming a hurricane after her."
5. "Bruce Forsyth is known as the king of the one-liners. That's because he has trouble remembering two lines."

LITERAL

1. "Their eyes met across a crowded room. It was her bedroom; she was a very popular girl."
2. "This fellow got sacked for rubbing people up the wrong way. He was a masseur."
3. "Whoever said figures don't lie never considered breast implants."
4. "It's true that men don't cry. Except when they're trying to assemble a flat pack from IKEA."
5. "The way to a man's heart is through his stomach. That was first said by an inexperienced surgeon."

MALAPROPISM

1. David Milliband.
2. Bruce Forsyth.
3. Seychelles.
4. Mauritius.
5. Aquarius

MENTAL PICTURE

1. "Certain people should avoid doing certain things. Like Dolly Parton taking up the accordion."
2. "The economy is going up and down like Dolly Parton on a trampoline."

3. "Clinton never brought his country to its knees, except for Monica Lewinsky."
4. "The good thing about those tiny Smart cars is you don't need a parking space. You just hook them on to your charm bracelet."
5. "He put on clean underwear every day. By the end of the week, he could hardly get his trousers on."

POLITICAL

1. "I heard of an M.P. that was burgled three times. Once for each of his homes."
2. "George Bush told his secretary ' If there is any trouble anywhere in the world I want to be woken up immediately. Even if I'm in a cabinet meeting.' "
3. "Lots of good things have been said about Gordon Brown. I know, because he was the one that said them."
4. "Gordon Brown can be credited with creating two million new jobs. Mostly in China, India and Japan."
5. "Ex-President Clinton admits he's had several love affairs. But his life is an open book, which you can buy at any bookstore in a plain brown wrapper."

PUNS

1. "Even riding stables are saying their customers are falling off."
2. "For Christmas my wife bought me a smoking jacket. Took me two and a half hours to put it out."
3. "The man who insisted on being cremated was just making an ash of himself."
4. "My plumber said last year's business was flush, but now it's down the drain."
5. "The lovebird left his mate because the *Trill* had gone."

RIDDLES

1. "Name five things that contain milk? Answer: Cheese, butter and three cows."

2. "Why are some people great fans of Red China? Answer: It looks lovely on a blue tablecloth."

3. "Why did the widow bury her tyrannical husband twelve feet under? Answer: Because deep down he was a good man."

4. "Before a farmer starts milking, what does he have to do? Answer: Make sure it's a cow."

5. "According to statistics, what's the longest a couple have ever been engaged? Answer: Depends what they're engaged in."

RHETORICAL QUESTIONS.

1. "Will they ever stamp out Flamenco dancing?"
2. "If all the world's a stage, where are the dressing rooms?"
3. "Why do they bother putting four wheels on supermarket trolleys when only three of them ever work?"
4. "Was the man who trained his rabbit to service 25 females a day, just trying to make a fast buck?"
5. "Did the man who paid too much for his Sushi get a raw deal?"

THE VERNACULAR

1. "A dentist married a manicurist. They've been fighting tooth and nail ever since."
2. "A salesman working on commission told his barber to take 15% off the top."
3. "Old Ma Kettle had four kids. Two with spouts and two without."
4. "So many petrol garages are closing it's getting impossible to fuel all the people all the time."
5. "Twiggy's considering having a boob job because she wants to make a mountain out of a mole hill."

SELF DEPRECATION

1. "My wife says she made a mistake when we got married. She says she'd have done better keeping the bouquet and throwing away the groom."

2. "My wife says I remind her of a whisky bottle. She says we're both empty from the neck up."
3. "You too can have a body like mine, unless you're prepared to take care of yourself."
4. "I performed my act to a room full of sick people. Mind you, they were well enough before I performed."
5. "They say my act appeals mostly to the 18 to 30 group. That's not their age, it's their I.Q."

Your exercise for this lesson is to create at least one gag (but hopefully more) in each of the gag forms I've displayed.

LESSON TWO – How to Create a Comedy Routine

There are hundreds of comedians working regularly in comedy clubs, all trying to become famous. But most of them will never be household names because they are not original enough. They do not have their own style or unique approach to comedy.

Many start by raiding gag books and end up doing the same jokes as each other. Jokes that the audience will have already heard last week and will probably hear again next week. These guys are often great at delivering the jokes, but haven't the faintest idea how to create new material. That's why comedy writers are so important. Comedians need us if they want to further their careers. Unless we are performers ourselves willing to hit the road doing one-night stands, we need those ambitious comedians as much as they need us.

What makes a comedian unique? The answer is simple. It's his/her approach to comedy. Here are examples of several well known British and American comedians with some of the gags that earned them to the top of their league.

WOODY ALLEN:

When I was kidnapped my parents sprang into action. They rented out my room.

If only God would give me a clear sign. Like making a large deposit in my name in a Swiss bank.

ROSEANNE BARR:

I've been married fourteen years and I have three kids. Obviously I breed well in captivity.

The way I feel, if the kids are still alive when my husband gets home from work, I've done my job.

JACK BENNY:

I had my choice tonight of buying a hundred-dollar ticket or being up here on the dais. So, good evening ladies and gentlemen.

I'm living in a very modest place. I have a room overlooking beautiful Claridges Hotel. I thought it was better than paying Claridges prices and overlooking the dump I'm in.

TOMMY COOPER:

Two cannibals eating a clown. One says to the other "Does this taste funny to you?"

I went into a pet shop. I said, "Can I buy a goldfish?" The guy said, "Do you want an aquarium?" I said, "I don't care what star sign it is."

RONNIE CORBETT:

My first romance was with a girl named Ethel Hardboard, she was thin but useful. We did our courting in a cemetery - me standing on a headstone and her with one foot in a grave.

Statistics show that if a small man and a large man are attacked by a certain virus at the same time, the large man will be sitting up drinking his *Lucozade* and reading his *Beano* at the same time as the small man's relations are sitting around drinking his sherry and reading his will.

JIMMY CRICKET:

My car broke down so I rang up the A.A. He said, "Your gasket's blew." I said, "What colour should it be?"

I rang up the local paper and said, "What do you charge for adverts?" He said, "£5 an inch." I said, "That's too expensive." He said, "Why? What are you advertising?" I said, "A 25 foot ladder."

RODNEY DANGERFIELD:

When I was a kid, all I knew was rejection. My yo-yo never came back.

You know when you're getting old, there are certain signs. I walked past a cemetery and two guys ran after me with shovels.

PHYLLIS DILLER:

I'm looking for a perfume to overpower men – I'm sick of karate.

I put on a peek-a-boo blouse. He peeked and booed.

PETER KAY:

I rang up British Telecom. I said, "I want to report a nuisance caller". He said, "Not you again."

So I went down to the local supermarket. I said, "I want to make a complaint, this vinegar's got lumps in it." He said, "Those are pickled onions."

STEVE MARTIN:

I love a woman with a head on her shoulders. I hate necks.

Do you know how many polyesters died to make this shirt?

GROUCHO MARX:

(TO A GOOD LOOKING GIRL) I wish you'd keep my hands to yourself.

Outside of a dog, a book is man's best friend. Inside of a dog, it's too dark to read.

JACKIE MASON:

I have no fear of Frank Sinatra. I told him, "Drop dead, you low-life bastard. You mean nothing to me." Thank God he wasn't there at the time.

My best friend is a guy half Italian, half Jewish. If he can't buy it wholesale, he steals it.

EMO PHILIPS:

I got some new underwear today. Well, new to me.

Probably the toughest time in anyone's life is when you have to murder a loved one because they're the devil. Other than that, it's been a good day.

JOAN RIVERS:

My mother never told me about the birds and bees. She figured I was so ugly I'd never need to know.

Prince Charles. Those ears! He could play ping pong without a paddle.

RITA RUDNER:

I love to shop after a bad relationship. I buy a new outfit and it makes me feel better. Sometimes if I really see a great outfit, I'll break up with someone on purpose.

My husband and I are either going to buy a dog or have a child. We can't decide whether to ruin our carpet or ruin our lives.

JERRY SEINFELD:

I have a friend who collects unemployment insurance. This guy has never worked so hard in his life as he has to keep this thing going. He's down there every week, waiting on the lines and getting interviewed and making up all those lies about looking for jobs. If they had any idea of the effort an energy that he is expending to avoid work, I'm sure they'd give him a raise.

What would the world be like if people said whatever they were thinking, all the time, whenever it came to them? How long would a blind date last? About 13 seconds, I think, "Oh, sorry, your rear end is too big." "That's O.K., your breath stinks anyway. See you later."

STEVEN WRIGHT:

I remember turning from one year old to two years old. I was real upset, because I figured in one year my age doubled. If this keeps up, by the time I'm six I'll be ninety.

I was walking down the street wearing glasses when my prescription ran out.

HENNY YOUNGMAN:

My wife will buy anything that's marked down. Last year she bought an elevator.

Playing golf the other day I broke 70. That's a lot of clubs.

As you read those gags you should actually be able to picture the comedians saying them. That's the key to writing for specific performers. Try to match their rhythm of speech so that you can imagine them confidently facing a paying audience with your carefully crafted material.

Until Dave Allen came on the scene most British comedians just told one unconnected joke after another. Dave, with the help of his two main writers Peter Vincent and Austin Steele, put gags related to a subject into a routine. As a writer it makes sense for you to do that because whereas you might get just £10 for a single gag, for a

38

routine you'd get paid by the minute. During Dave's Allen's regime the BBC were paying writers £100 per minute. His routines usually lasted about three minutes.

So how do you set about writing a routine? The first step is to pick a subject and create as many single gags as you can. Then select about a dozen of them strung together into a workable routine so that each gag leads to the next. I say about a dozen because some comedians have a slower delivery than others. Bob Hope for instance aimed at six gags a minute, but George Burns only did three.

In the last lesson we explored the topic of MARRIAGE for its gag potential. This time we'll go for two more universal subjects. A universal subject is one that is familiar to everyone. Our subjects will be CARS and SPORTS.

Starting with CARS we need to list everything we can think of that has a connection . Here are a few:

Speed... Traffic... Petrol... Seat Belts... Road Tax... Insurance... Gears... Sat Navs... Passengers... Mileage... Repairs... Tyres... Hubcaps... Traffic Lights... Brakes... M.O.T.s... Reckless Driving... Parking... Parking Meters... Parking Tickets... Parking Fines... One Way Streets... Motorways... Towing Away... The Car Pound... Driving Licence... Driving Test... Taxis... Taxi Drivers... Taxi Routes... Odometer... Taxi Fare Metre... The Bonnet... Steering Wheel... Handbrake... Log Book... Engine Knocking... Exhaust Pipe... The Boot... Glove Compartment... Ashtray... Cigarette Lighter... Headlamps... Fog Light... Dipped Lights... Hazard Lights... Hand Signals.

We probably have enough ideas to work on. Now we have to pick out those that have a potential for comedy. Not all the gags we'll come up with will fit into the finished routine, even though they may be stronger than some we will use. The point is that they have to naturally follow one another. Each gag should lead the way to the next one.

Here are some possible thoughts on EXAGGERATION:

I've had so many parking fines, they're thinking of giving me a season ticket.

The speedometer had been turned back so far it had Roman numerals.

The car's so old the insurance policy covers fire, theft and Viking raids.

The spare tyre was almost completely bald. I've seen more rubber on the end of a pencil.

I bought a classic model. So high class the radiator was filled with Perrier.

I'm now in my fourth year paying off the car. Two more years and I'll own the hubcaps.

The traffic jam on the M25 was so bad, I stopped to change a flat tyre and still kept my place in line.

My cousin's so rich he has four cars. One for each direction.

His car's so big he keeps his spare tyre in the glove compartment.

His car's so big it takes him two hours to go through a 5 minute car wash.

Next we'll look for WORD PLAYS:

As the great Bard might have said "Parking is such street sorrow."

They told me it was a get-a-way car. That's true. The previous owner couldn't wait to get away from it.

She keeps the A.A. and R.A.C. on their tows.

On my last car I paid cash for everything except the battery. That I had charged.

The car has an independent horn. It doesn't give a hoot.

I sent for the breakdown service. When the mechanic saw my car, he broke down.

I think of my car as a Rolls, because every time I leave it on an incline it rolls downhill.

The dealer gave me what they call in the trade a "Nudist Guarantee" – Nothing's covered.

I asked the mechanic what service my car needed. He said a memorial.

I've never been pinched for going too fast. Mind you, I've been slapped a few times.

Now on to ASSUMPTION form:

I bought a real dud. I phoned the A.A, and they were very helpful. They sent round a dustcart.

I drove into a service station and said, "I want a new tyre for this car." The mechanic said, "Sounds like a fair exchange to me."

Somebody actually complimented me on my driving today. They left a note on my windscreen says "Parking fine."

Congratulate me, I've just gone into partnership with NatWest Bank. They own half my car.

I was trying to get a new car for my wife, but nobody would swap.

My new car is expensive, but at least it gets me where I'm going. To the bank for a loan.

So far I've paid for three cars: My doctor's, my dentist's and my plumber's.

My car goes from 0 to 60 in ten seconds. Not miles, feet.

How about IMPLIED?

It was so old it was actually made in England.

The police use a lot of unmarked cars. Do you know what an unmarked car is? One that my wife hasn't driven yet.

I only use the car for show. When I'm in a hurry, I walk.

I turned up late, but it wasn't my fault. I was behind a used-car salesman at confession.

What my wife doesn't know about driving could fill a hospital.

Every time my car passes a scrap yard it gets homesick.

My wife learnt to drive at the Kamikaze Driving School.

Here are some other gags about cars that don't necessarily fit into any forms, but may well slip nicely into a routine:

Today what most Londoners pray for when they go to church is a parking space.

The only exercise drivers get now is the long walk back to their car.

In the old days you could hire a car for a week for what it now costs to park one for a day.

Since I've taken to buying used cars I've realised that while figures don't lie, car salesmen certainly do.

It was so old the only thing that didn't make a noise was the horn.

It was the kind of car you'd call flattery, because you know it won't get you anywhere.

It was safe to leave on the street at night. Vandals thought someone else had beaten them to it.

I finally got rid of it at a toll booth. When the attendant said, "Two pounds." I said, "Done!"

I never washed it. I had it dry cleaned.

The car was able to cruise at 100 miles per hour. Fast enough to get from London to Leeds in just two hours and four speeding tickets.

I really do feel they should abolish the 70 mph speed limit on motorways. What annoys me most is that I often get stuck behind someone that obeys it.

I think the speed limit should be raised to 80. That way, drivers who now do 90 will speed up to 100. They'll get home faster and leave the roads safer for the rest of us.

My wife thinks I'm a lousy driver. After a few miles I always turn to her and say, "Look, dear, let's change roles. From now on YOU drive and I'LL nag!"

A lot of drivers don't need seatbelts so much as straightjackets.

The main reason women are more careful drivers is, if they're involved in a crash, newspapers print their age.

A cousin of mine made a fortune in the motor industry. He makes toupées for bald tyres.

If you drive like hell, that's where you'll wind up.

Isn't it funny how women can squeeze into tiny corsets, but not into parking spaces?

I still remember when the only problem with parking was getting the girl to agree.

Did you hear about the playboy who bought a Ferrari because it guaranteed him more girls to the mile?

More people are getting cars. And the way some of them drive more cars are getting people.

There's no doubt a small car reduces your problem of finding a parking space. But it also increases your problem of finding your car.

There must be something wrong with the steering in my wife's car. This morning she missed 2 pedestrians.

She had three accidents just taking the written test.

People in London don't give hand signals any more. They daren't. You put your arm out and someone'll steal your watch.

I don't know how much petrol my car holds. I've never had enough money to fill the tank.

This sat nav thing is nothing new. I've had a woman telling me where to go for ages.

You can buy one of those sports cars that drive really fast. They come with a log book, a manual and a form to fill out your will.

Toyota now sell you two cars at the same time. That's so you've got one to drive while they recall the other.

The warranty lasts for two years, or until something goes wrong.

Even the ashtrays don't work.

Things change in the car industry. It used to be if you wanted to swear at another driver you had to roll down the window. Now you can just phone him.

If I were to prepare a routine on CARS here's what it might look like:

As the great Bard might have said, "Parking is such sweet sorrow." Today what most Londoners pray for when they go to church is a parking space. Drivers complain the only exercise they get now is the long walks to where they left the car. And if you do find a car park, it's expensive. I still remember the time when you could hire a car for a week for what it costs to park one for a day. I've had so many parking fines they're thinking of giving me a season ticket.

In recent years I've taken to only buying second hand cars. It's taught me that while figures don't lie, used car salesmen often do. One salesman confidentially whispered, "This was a get-a-way car." And it was. The previous owner couldn't wait to get away from it. It was so old the only thing that didn't make a noise was the horn. The meter had been turned back that far the figures were in Roman numerals. It was the kind of car you'd call flattery because you knew it wouldn't get you anywhere.

Unfortunately I'm no expert. In my time I've bought some real duds. One was such a wreck, when I phoned the AA for a tow they sent a dustcart. The spare tyre was worn down. I've seen more rubber on the end of a pencil. I drove it into a service station and said, "I want a new tyre for this car." They said, "That sounds like a fair exchange." The only good thing about that car was it was safe to leave in the street overnight. Vandals thought someone else had beaten them to it. I finally got rid of it at a toll booth. When the attendant said, "Two pounds." I said, "Done" and left it there.

Next one I bought was a sleek sports car. A real classic model. So high class you had to fill the radiator with Perrier. I never washed it. I had it dry cleaned. That car was able to cruise at 100 miles an hour. Fast enough to get from London to Leeds in just two hours and four speeding tickets.

I really do feel they should abolish the 70 m.p.h. limit on motorways. What annoys me most is that I occasionally get stuck behind someone who obeys it. I think it should be raised to 80. That way drivers who now do 90 will speed up to 100. They'll get home faster and leave the roads safer for the rest of us. Mind you, my wife thinks I'm a lousy driver anyway. After a few miles I always turn to her and say, "Look dear, let's swap roles. From now on YOU drive and I'LL nag."

Now we'll move on to our other subject, SPORT. There are so many different sports you have ample scope to find twelve gags for your routine. Most popular sport in Britain is FOOTBALL, so let's start listing associated words:

Pitch... Goalposts... Referee... Ref's whistle... Half time.. Ref's Assistants... Off-side... Throw in... Penalty... Free kick... Foul... Corners... Dribbling... Passing... Goalkeeper... Striker... Centre forward... Forwards... Half backs... Backs... Defenders... Into touch... Heading the ball... Tackling... Football managers... Sven Ericksson... Abramovich... Arsenal... Spurs... Cup Final... Various leagues... Alex Ferguson... Arsene Wenger... UEFA... World Cup... Wembley... Millennium Stadium... High Wages... Rooney... Crouch... Lampard... Transfer fees... Dressing rooms... The tunnel... Substitutes... On the bench

I don't think it is necessary to singly categorise each gag. By now the thinking behind them should be obvious to you. I'll just run through some of the gag possibilities that football presents to a comedy writer:

This season Portsmouth (or whoever) played so badly, when they had a throw in it should have been the towel.

It's not fair. Footballers are paid all that money and yet they're still awarded free kicks.

They call them managers, but most of them can't even manage to keep their job.

Football is our number two sport – after sex.

A woman at the football match kept shouting, "Shoot the Referee! Shoot the Referee!" She turned out to be the Referee's wife.

Referees are what footballers become when their eyesight is failing.

At school the teacher asked, "Can anyone tell me where Southgate is?" Little Johnny said, "Yes, he's at Wembley playing for Manchester United."

My wife was excited when Arsenal announced they had a new striker. She thought they said streaker.

I was in the school soccer team. I started out as halfback and wound up as drawback.

He couldn't even pass the salt at dinner time.

Unless they buck up their ideas it looks like the Gunners are going to be goners.

They haven't a league to stand on. If Portsmouth *are* relegated, they won't have a league to stand on.

Of course footballers are highly paid. None of them would do it for kicks.

If foreigners want to come to England they needn't smuggle through France. Just become footballers.

It's as rare as a Briton in the Arsenal team.

(NAME OF PLAYERS) were on the bench so much they've got cauliflower rears.

(NAME OF PLAYER)'s been on the bench longer than The Lord Chief Justice.

In tennis they lob… In football they gob.

Next most popular sport is probably GOLF. Here are some associated words to plough through:

The golf ball... Golf bag... Various clubs... Golf tee... Slice... Hook... Fairway... Putting... Greens... Scoring... Birdies... Eagles... The albatross... Par... The Open... The golf range... The Masters... The swing... The stance... The Club Professional... The flag... The hole/cup... The 19th hole... Bunkers... Fore!... Play through... Golf cart... Spiked shoes... Lying about scores... Swearing... Slow and fast greens... Golf outfits... One glove... Plus fours...

Now here come the golf gags:

Golf is the game for people who are good at saving their health and losing their temper.

Golf keeps you on the green, in the pink and in the red.

A golfer is a gardener digging up someone else's lawn.

A golf ball is something a man chases when he's too old to chase anything else.

I shoot golf in the low seventies. When it gets any colder I stay home.

Golf. I've seen better slices in a loaf of bread.

I was known as the unhappy hooker.

A lying golfer is someone who shouts, "Fore!" hits six and puts down five.

When Palmer beat Faldo for the fifth time he said, "Don't worry Nick, you'll be burying me soon." And Faldo said, "Yes, but even then it'll be your hole."

My wife's so used to bidding at auctions, when we're at golf and I shout, "Fore!" she shouts, "Four and a half!"

I played golf with Ronnie Corbett... On miniature golf, of course. Ronnie never shouted, "Fore!" For him it was three and a half.

I developed a backward swing that got me a big following. Mostly sailors.

My golf was so bad, whenever I played they lowered the flags to half mast.

I dug up so much turf they made me an honorary archaeologist.

I spent more time in the bunker that Adolph Hitler.

The golf Pro. told me I'd benefit by keeping my head down. And he was right. I found lots of golf balls.

Woosnam's ball hit a spectator who threatened to sue for a million pounds. Woosnam apologised "I meant to say, "Fore!" And the spectator said, "Alright, four million."

The doctor advised me to give up golf. He said at my age it was dangerous going near an open hole.

Tiger Woods was one for the ladies. Apparently he scored even better off the course than on.

Let's now consider what TENNIS can offer for comedy. Starting, as always, with our association list:

Courts... Nets... Balls... Scores... Love... Game, set & match... Murray mania... Deuce... Backhand... Volley... Forehand... Smash... Grand slam... Wimbledon... Tramlines... In... Out... Baseline... Drop shot... Set point... Match point... Umpire... Murray... New balls... Lob... Coach... Contempt of court... Settled out of court... It was in court so he was caught out... He said it was net and the Russian said it was *niet*.

I remember my first game of tennis. How green was my volley.

The way I played they were going to sue me for contempt of court.

My wife told our doctor that I'd got Murray mania. He said not to worry; it never reaches the final stage.

John McEnroe argued with his wife on their wedding night. He insisted it was in.

Wimbledon Tennis Club made a net profit.

He used a forward hand to win, and then the Mafia gave him a backhand to lose.

He was more seedy than seeded.

McEnroe is now a commentator. He's at Wimbledon more often than the Wombles.

He won't play Dolly Parton any more. She always winds up two points in front.

He was their number one player. And you can't get much lower than one.

McEnroe's the one that gave the umpire the 'ump

It's not exactly racquet science.

Next we'll try DARTS:

Here's a list of possible thoughts for gags on this subject:

Dartboard... the oche... Beer bellies... Double to start and finish... Scores... The darts/feathers... Bulls eye... Jocky Wilson... Keith Duller.

Jocky Wilson was known as Mr. 180. That wasn't his score it was his waist size.

They put Jocky on the weighing machine and he sucked in his tummy. The doctor said, "That won't help you." He said, "Yes it will. Now I can see the numbers."

He was so fat, Jocky never saw the oche.

They told me I had to start with a double. So I went and had a double and by the time I got back the game was over.

I wanted to play darts, but I didn't have the figure for it.

There are many other sports to poke fun at, such as cricket, boxing, fencing, wrestling, rugby, skating and ski-ing. A routine on SPORT might be written along the following lines:

I have always been a great lover of sports. Even as a school kid I used to play hooky to play hockey. I was in the school soccer team till they tried me out as half back and discovered I was more of a drawback.

I tried every competitive sport going. Even tiddly winks, where I was disqualified for being too tiddly. Darts was my next choice, but I didn't have the figure for it. My idol was Jocky Wilson, the man they called "Mr. 180". Nothing to do with his score. It was just the size of his waistline. Once, when Jocky decided to go on diet, the doctor put him on a weighing machine and he immediately sucked in his tummy. The doctor said, "That won't help you." And Jocky said, "Yes, it will. Now I can see the numbers." In all those years of playing, Jocky never saw the oche.

At one time I fancied myself as another Lawrence Dallaglio. Mainly because the rugby player pulled all the girls. They were mad about his tackle. My next fancy was golf. My first game was with little Ronnie Corbett. On a miniature golf course. Ronnie had special dispensation. When he hit the ball he only had to shout "Three and a half!"

After a few games I developed a backswing that got me quite a following, mostly from sailors. To be honest, I was never much good at golf. In fact, I was so bad that when I entered the course they lowered the flags to half mast. With every stroke I dug up so much turf they made me an honorary archaeologist. Golfers will understand when I say my most used club was the sand wedge. Each ball went straight into the sand. I spent so much time in the bunker I was getting mail addressed to Hitler. Even to this day I can't bear to look at an egg timer.

I did try to improve my game; I took lessons from a professional. I'd mention his name, but he's paid me not to. His main advice was "If you keep your head down it'll pay off." It did. I found a lot of lost golf balls. Perhaps it's not surprising I don't get invited to tee anymore. However, I do still watch the game and was there when an Ian Woosnam ball hit a spectator right in the face. The angry man shouted, "I'm going to sue you for five million!" Woosenam shouted back, "I did say 'Fore'" And the man said, "Alright, I'll accept four million."

I once harboured an ambition to get into the England cricket team, but they've enough useless players already. I think they'd do better giving up Lords and moving to Lourdes.

It's the same with our England football team. I saw their last game. I thought when they got a throw-in, it should have been the towel. They badly need a good manager but it seems the one thing most football managers can't manage these days is to keep their jobs.

My wife's a great football fan and when Arsene Wenger said he was going to play a new "striker" she couldn't wait to get to the match. She thought he said "streaker."

Our tennis players do us no credit either. The way some of them play they should be had up for contempt of court. I heard of one fanatical tennis-watcher who was so obsessed his wife took him to a psychiatrist. She said "My husband's got Henmanitis" The medic said "Not to worry, it never reaches the final stage."

What I'd like you to do as your exercise for Lesson Two is string 12 gags together on both subjects, CARS and SPORTS so they are linked into two routines. You can either use the gags I have given you or choose your own or a mixture of yours and mine. If you can suggest a comedian they may be suitable for, that would be a bonus, but at this stage it isn't essential.

LESSON THREE - Black-Outs, Quickies And Sketches.

Over the past decade comedy has undergone a huge change. Sketches used to last as long as eight minutes on screen. That has now been whittled down to just two and a half minutes. The reason? Viewers no longer have that attention span. This makes it harder for the sketch writer, who now has to squeeze a beginning, middle and end into a much shorter a time. Often it means employing a set up for your sketch that allows you to start in the middle. I'll make that point more clearly when we get to writing sketches.

BLACK-OUTS

Black-outs are quick gags that usually do not require a specific set, but often necessitate using a prop. I'll assume you are already familiar with the old vaudeville Black-out where a monologue is interrupted by a man walking across stage carrying a suitcase. "Where are you going?" asks the monologist and gets the reply "I'm taking my case to court." Seconds later he is interrupted by the same man who returns carrying a ladder. "What now?" "I'm going to a higher court."

My first successful Black-out had a Monk walking to the centre of an empty stage singing, "If you were the only girl in the world…" At that point a Nun joins him and sings, "And you were the only boy…" There's a slight pause then together they sing, "Nothing!" It earned its laugh because everyone knows of their celibacy vows.

Black-outs, however, have become old fashioned and are seldom used these days, except in end-of-the-pier revue shows. So let's move swiftly on to Quickies.

QUICKIES

Quickies are miniature sketches that last anything from 15 seconds to one minute. They will be a set up, visually or verbally, to a single big laugh at the end. I bought hundreds of Quickies from new writers during my four year tenure as Comedy Consultant to Samstag Nacht, the very popular German TV Saturday night satirical series and my days as Script Editor at BBC TV, Thames TV and Yorkshire TV.

Here are some examples of Quickies:

A woman being wheeled on a stretcher into a Maternity Ward tells the ambulance man, "No, it's the wrong ward. I want Accident & Emergency. My finger's stuck in this bowling ball." She opens her coat to reveal that what looked like a belly bulge is in fact a bowling ball with her finger lodged in it.

A boxer climbs into the ring and removes his dressing gown and shows a tattooed face of an old woman on his chest with the word *mother* beneath it. He looks terrified as he sees the huge figure of his opponent and explains to the referee, "I'm not sentimental. I'm just hoping he won't hit a woman."

A husband and his ugly wife are having a picnic near the edge of a cliff. They have been eating chicken and he finds the wishbone. They each grab an end of it as he says, "Make a wish." The wife makes a silent wish and then pulls on the wishbone which breaks, sending her rolling backwards over the cliff edge. The husband looks over the cliff edge and, with a satisfied smile says, "Well, I got MY wish."

Two armed policemen are wearing flak jackets and pointing their revolvers at something off screen. One of the policemen shouts, "Alright, the game's up, we know you're in there. You'd better give yourself up. Throw your gun out the window and come out with your arms in the air, Shorty!" Camera widens the angle to show he is shouting to a kid's dolls house.

In Deadwood Gulch cowboy town we focus on a door marked "HANK SMITH – DOCTOR". Fade through to the Doctor's Waiting Room where five patients have been shot dead and are lying in various positions. The doctor opens the door and says, "Who's next?" A cowboy with a pistol in his hand, replies, "Me, Doc, What can you give me for an itchy trigger finger?"

A man is at the bar in a Pub. His wife bursts in and angrily shouts at him, "I thought I'd find you here! You promised me faithfully you'd given up drinking!" He replies, "I almost have. As you can see I'm down to one a day." Camera angle widens to show he has huge glass of beer on the counter in front of him.

Six men wearing their football kit are seated at a table eating their dinner. The one on one end shouts to his mate on the other end, "Would you pass the salt please, Bert?" Bert says, "Sure." He climbs on the table and passes the salt by kicking it across.

A man at the bar of a Pub is asked by the barman, "What'll you have?" He says, "I'll have a beer." Barman says, "And what about your friend here?" The man replies, "Nothing for him, thanks. He's tapering off." Camera angle now includes second man who wears a suit that's very wide at the shoulders but narrows as it gets down to his shoes.

A man seated in a theatre keeps moving his head from side to side because his view is blocked by a column. He complains and is told that his ticket clearly stated it was a restricted view and that he would have to pay another £5 if he wanted to see more clearly. Reluctantly he hands over his £5 and the manager just physically picks up the column and takes it away.

In Amsterdam's famous red light district a prostitute is leaning seductively against a street lamp post. Two other prostitutes are posing in a window behind her. A man comes along, sees the two waving to him, but ignores them and walks off with the one at the lamp post. One of the disappointed girls turns to the other and says, "Ah well, I guess he prefers the outdoor type."

If you are submitting comedy material to a foreign country you must be sure they are au fait with the subject you are hoping to amuse them with. Here is a Quickie that was rejected by my German TV producer. After you have read it, I will explain why.

SHERLOCK HOLMES & DR. WATSON

LIVING ROOM OF FLAT. NIGHT.

A WOMAN IS PACING NERVOUSLY BACK AND FORTH.
THERE'S A LOUD KNOCK ON THE DOOR.

WOMAN RUNS TO THE DOOR AND SPEAKS.

WOMAN:

Who is it?

HOLMES: (OUT OF VISION)

It's Sherlock Holmes and Doctor Watson.

WOMAN:

(OPENS DOOR) Oh good, you finally got here.

SHERLOCK HOLMES AND DR. WATSON ENTER.

HOLMES:

How do you do, Madam? This is Dr. Watson and he's told me everything.

WATSON:

(TO WOMAN) How do you do? Now you're sure you left everything just as it was when I talked to you on the phone?

WOMAN:

Yes, I've touched nothing. Nothing at all.

HOLMES:

(GOING TO FIRST CUPBOARD) Alright Watson. Let's inspect the room.

WATSON:

Very good, Holmes.

HOLMES OPENS CUPBOARD DOOR. A BODY FALLS OUT OF IT AND LANDS IN A HEAP ON THE FLOOR.

HOLMES:

Ah hah ...just as I thought.

THEY STEP OVER THE BODY AND PROCEED TO THE NEXT CUPBOARD.

WATSON:

Shall I open this one, Holmes?

HOLMES:

Yes, Watson, please do.

WATSON OPENS THE CUPBOARD AND ANOTHER BODY FALLS OUT.

HOLMES:

(STEPPING OVER BODY) Another one. Hmmm. Let's have a look over here.

HOLMES OPENS THE THIRD CUPBOARD. YET ANOTHER BODY FALLS OUT.

HOLMES:

Ah ha, that makes three.

WOMAN:

What do you think, Mr. Holmes?

HOLMES:

(LOOKING AROUND) Well, it's got ample cupboard space. I think we'll take it, eh Watson.

HOLMES TAKES WALLET OUT OF HIS POCKET AND IS ABOUT TO HAND MONEY OVER TO THE WOMAN

What did you say the rent was?

It had worked very well on British TV, but the producer decided that Sherlock Holmes and Doctor Watson were not well enough known to his German audience.

On the other hand, here is a sketch that did succeed in that country because, though the characters, in this instance, had German names they could easily be changed to suit most countries.

AIR TRAFFIC CONTROL SKETCH

THE TWO SETS ARE A SMALL SECTION OF THE AIR TRAFFIC CONTROL ROOM OF A SMALL AIRFIELD AND THE COCKPIT OF A SMALL SINGLE ENGINE PLANE FLYING IN A THICK FOG. WE INTERCUT BETWEEN THE TWO SETS AT THE TV DIRECTOR'S DISCRETION. WE START IN THE CONTROL TOWER WHERE GRETA IS ALONE IN FRONT OF A RADAR SCREEN. SHE IS BORED AND POLISHING HER FINGERNAILS.

SUDDENLY THE SILENCE IS BROKEN BY WALTER'S PANIC-STRICKEN VOICE OVER THE SPEAKER.

WALTER:(VOICE OVER)

May Day! May Day! This is an emergency. I'm lost in this thick fog. Can anyone down there help me?

GRETA STOPS POLISHING HER NAILS AND SWITCHES ON HER MICROPHONE.

GRETA:

Yes, I hear you. This is Noorheim Airfield. I can hear you. You're coming in loud and clear.

WALTER:

(RELIEVED) Thank God for that! This is Captain Giller in a single engine Comanche. I've been circling round for hours trying to find my way. Now I'm out of fuel and losing height. I need urgent assistance.

GRETA:

(RECOGNISES HIS VOICE) You said 'Captain Giller', would that be Captain Speedy Giller from Munich?

WALTER:

Yes. Why, do you know me?

GRETA:

This is Greta. (NO REACTION FROM HIM) Greta Bosscher. (STILL NO REACTION FROM HIM)…From Cologne. You don't remember me, do you? We spent a lovely weekend together in Bavaria. It was wonderful. So romantic.

WALTER:

(SHARPLY) Good, I'm glad you enjoyed it. Now could you please help me get down from here. Look on your radar screen and tell me my exact position.

GRETA:

No.

WALTER:

(SURPRISED) No? What do you mean 'no'?

GRETA:

I'm not talking to you. After that weekend you promised you'd call me, and you never did.

WALTER:

Well I'm calling you now.

GRETA:

Oh sure, you're calling me NOW. When it suits you! That's typical of you men. It's six years since that weekend and you never called me once.

WALTER:

(DESPERATELY MAKING AN EXCUSE) I meant to, but I er… lost your phone number.

GRETA:

You could have got it from the phone directory.

WALTER:

I lost their number as well. Look, this conversation is ridiculous. I'm running out of time up here.

GRETA:

Don't you even care that you left me with a broken heart?

WALTER:

Help me down safely and I'll buy you a transplant.

GRETA:

That's right, go on, make a joke of it! You don't care that I waited by that phone night after night and not one call.

WALTER:

I'll make it up to you. I'll call you twice tomorrow.

GRETA:

You don't care. You're not even sorry you didn't call.

WALTER:

I am now! Look Greta, I've lost a lot of altitude. I can't hold on much longer. Do your job. You're supposed to help pilots in distress.

GRETA:

Alright, I will.

WALTER:

(RELIEVED) Good.

GRETA:

(AFTER A PAUSE)....As soon as you say you're sorry.

WALTER:

I can't believe this is happening.

GRETA:

Say you're sorry or I'm switching off the microphone.

WALTER:

(GIVING IN) Alright, alright, I'm sorry. OK now?

GRETA:

No. You haven't said what you're sorry about.

WALTER:

I'm sorry it's you that picked up my distress call.

GRETA:

(THREATENING) I'm switching off the microphone.

WALTER:

(DESPERATE) No, no, don't do that, I'll SAY I'm sorry. I'm sorry I didn't call you after that weekend in…er, wherever it was.

GRETA:

Bavaria.

WALTER:

Yes, Bavaria.

GRETA:

You don't even remember it, do you?

WALTER:

It was six years ago.

GRETA:

I remember it so clearly. You called me by a pet name. Can you recall what name you called me then?

WALTER:

(ALMOST UNDER HIS BREATH) No, but I can think of a few to call you now! Look, I haven't time for these games. My whole life is flashing before my eyes. Maybe when it gets to that weekend in Bavaria I'll remember the name.

Please! Help me down, or the next call you get from me could be through a medium.

GRETA:

You called me Honeybun. Go on. Call me Honeybun again, the way you did then.

WALTER:

Alright, Honeybun. Now listen to me carefully, Honeybun. I'm in terrible trouble up here, Honeybun…and if you don't help me I'll never be able to call you Honeybun again, because in just a few minutes I'm going to crash.

GRETA:

You'll be alright.

WALTER:

Sure I'll be alright. Right up till the moment my plane hits the ground.

GRETA;

No, I mean it. The fog's clearing.

WALTER:

(RELIEVED) You're right, so it is. I can see your airfield directly below me. I'm safe. Thank God, I'm safe.

GRETA:

Here's your landing instructions. Turn to an angle of 160 degrees. (HE REPEATS THAT) Lower your undercarriage. (HE REPEATS THAT) Follow the arrow on runway three. (HE REPEATS THAT) Now over and out.

WALTER:

No, Greta, before you go I need to know one more thing.

GRETA:

What's that?

WALTER:

If you're free Friday night, do you fancy a weekend in Bavaria?

That's an example of what's known as The Panic Sketch, one of the many varied forms of sketches frequently used by comedy writers. Let's familiarize ourselves with some popular sketch forms. Here are just a dozen to start you off with:

THE PANIC SKETCH

That's when you get your lead character into a situation that is dangerous, embarrassing or just damned right awkward. Like a businessman who takes his sexy girlfriend to a hotel in Brighton for a dirty weekend. They turn out to be the hotel's thousandth customers and the manager has arranged for the local TV channel to interview them to mark the occasion. The man, in panic, has to use various dodges to hide his name, face and even disguise his voice so as not to be recognised.

THE REVERSE SKETCH

That's when you take a normal situation and do it from the opposite point of view. It could be proposing divorce as you would propose marriage. It could be men acting like women or vice versa. For instance a sketch based on the *Kon Tiki Expedition* with a woman explorer Thora Heyerdahl instead the male counterpart Thor Heyerdahl. Instead of charting her route planning food reserves, she'd be busy working out what clothes to pack for the journey.

THE SATIRICAL SKETCH

That's usually political. It is either sending up a person or an organisation. Having a politician on *Mastermind* giving evasive or ambiguous answers to every question would be classed as satire. Satirical writer Art Buchwald made a good living using everyday items from the news and taking them one step further. It's worth reading his many published books to see the master at work.

THE PASTICHE SKETCH

That's when you take a well known film, book or play and do your own version of it. Like Morecambe and Wise did their version of *Julius Caesar*, or Tommy Cooper playing *Henry VIII*, or Jimmy Cricket's *Robin Hood*. You imagine what Julius Caesar, King Henry and the Sherwood Forest outlaw would have been like if they had the characteristics of Eric Morecambe, Tommy Cooper or Jimmy Cricket and write your sketch accordingly.

THE INTERVIEW SKETCH

That's when an odd character is interviewed, which is exactly what it says it is. I remember seeing an American series where each week the mothers of fictional or historical characters were being interviewed. They included the mothers of Columbus, the Invisible Man and Al Capone. Also in the category would be Bob Newhart's interview with Sir Walter Raleigh about the invention of the cigarette. Or his quizzing the Wright Brothers about their first flight.

THE "WHAT IF" SKETCH

That's when the writer takes any well known situation and asks himself what would have happened if it went a different way. Like supposing Romeo and Juliet hadn't died, but actually got married. He would show what their marriage might be like on their 20th anniversary. The star crossed lovers would be arguing like mad. What if our country not only had a female Prime Minister but an all-women Parliament too? Parliamentary Question Time could be all questions about make-up, hair do's and current clothes fashion.

THE AUDIENCE KNOWS SKETCH

That's when the laughs come thick and fast because the audience know something the star of the sketch is ignorant of. Like the Tommy Cooper sketch in which the comedian flew to New York to appear in the *Ed Sullivan Show* on the same day as Henry Cooper, the heavyweight boxer flew there to fight Joe Baksi at Madison Square Garden. The driver sent to collect the boxer at the Kennedy Airport picks up the wrong "Mr. Cooper" and the confused Tommy finds himself stripped down to his shorts and led into the ring to fight. It's funny because he thinks it's part of the *Ed Sullivan Show*, while we the audience know it isn't.

THE FUNNY SET SKETCH

That's when the humour is built around the location where the sketch takes place. Two sketches immediately come to mind. The first is the *Forsyte Saga* sketch we did for Mike & Bernie Winters. In the real *Forsyte Saga* they buy a house that is built on a hill. So in our sketch we tilted the camera and gave the set a 45 degree slope and had Bernie, as the butler, trying to serve tea. He had to pull himself (with a rope) up and down the room and kept spilling the contents of his tray. Russ Abbot later did a very similar sketch where he played a waiter in the Tower of Pisa restaurant and had a very hard (and hilarious) time serving the meals.

THE VOICE-OVER SKETCH

That's when the characters in the sketch have little or no dialogue and an off screen narrator tells the audience what is going on. Benny Hill did several sketches where we were shown the torrid love scene in a foreign film while Benny's voice told us what the sexy lovers were supposedly saying to each other. It's like the old silent film days, but instead of captions a voice-over is used. You may also remember the sketch in which Benny's off screen voice described the clothes and models in a cat walk in a fashion parade.

THE DOMESTIC SKETCH

That's just about any sketch that involves a husband and wife and usually revolves around a situation in their home. A good example might be the Sid Caesar sketch where his wife (Imogene Coca) is desperately trying to butter him up with his favourite meal before breaking the news she has smashed up their new car. It could be as simple as two spouses arguing over where to go for their holiday.

THE "IF PEOPLE BEHAVED LIKE ANIMALS (OR VICE VERSA)" SKETCH

That's when you can come up with a convincing reason for a human to adopt the mannerisms of an animal. In a Carol Burnett show comedian Tim Conway accidentally injected himself with monkey gland liquid and desperately tried to hide his strange ape-like actions and noises in an interview with his prospective father-in-law. Morecambe and Wise did several sketches dressed up as birds or insects and spoke in the vernacular of those creatures.

THE "THINGS GOING WRONG" SKETCH

That's when the comedy is based on props not working as they should, or doors or windows not opening. A typical sketch in this genre had a safety curtain stuck halfway up so that only the lower halves of the actors were visible to the audience. Another sketch had a hypochondriac doing an intimate love scene but keeping a safe distance from the woman for fear of catching any germs. The sound system going awry or the actors' voices being out of sync. also come into this category.

Sketches need to be written in the recognised style of the show or performers. The Two Ronnies, Barker and Corbett, had their own distinctive speech rhythms. Here's a sketch in which you should be able to mentally picture Ronnie Barker as the doctor and Ronnie Corbett as the patient.

PAINFUL VISIT TO THE DOCTOR:

DOCTOR'S SURGERY. MORNING

THE SHORT SIGHTED DOCTOR IS SEATED AT HIS DESK AS RONNIE (A PATIENT) ENTERS.

DOCTOR:

Good morning Mrs. Smith.

RONNIE:

(CORRECTING HIM) Mr. Smith, Doctor.

DOCTOR:

If you say so. Now then Mr. Smith-Doctor, what seems to be the trouble?

RONNIE:

It's my throat, doctor.

DOCTOR:

Your throat, you say? How long have you had it?

RONNIE:

I've always had it. It came with my body. It's part of a set.

DOCTOR:

I see. And what exactly do you think is wrong with your throat?

RONNIE:

I think it's tonsillitis. An inflammation of the membranous tissue surrounding the tonsil. I have high fever and a headache.

DOCTOR:

I see. Would you mind taking your trousers off? I want to have a look at your feet. Tonsillitis, indeed. Show me the right foot.

RONNIE:

(DROPS TROUSERS) The right foot? Is that facing me or away from me?

DOCTOR:

Don't be silly. If it was away from you, you wouldn't be able to walk. You'd be hopping all over the place. (LOOKS AT RONNIE'S RIGHT FOOT) Now take off your sock. (HE DOES SO) Oh dear me. I thought as much. Mmmm.

RONNIE:

Is it anything serious?

DOCTOR:

I'm afraid you'll never play football again.

RONNIE:

I don't play football. I don't even like football.

DOCTOR:

That's just as well, because you won't miss it.

RONNIE:

Doctor, it's my throat I want examined, not my foot. (SUDDENLY WORRIED) Can the two things be connected?

DOCTOR:

(LAUGHING) Oh dear me, no. You'd look a bit funny with your throat connected to your foot. No, I'm afraid you've got it wrong. It's tonsillitis, nothing to do with the feet at all.

RONNIE:

(PATRONISING HIM) I'm sorry, doctor. I didn't mean to mislead you.

DOCTOR:

You'd better pop into hospital and have the old appendix out, just to be on the safe side. Can't have you collapsing all over the place with appendicitis. (AS AN AFTERTHOUGHT) Oh, and I'll give you something for those feet of yours.

RONNIE:

(PUZZLED) Something for my feet? What can you give me for my feet?

DOCTOR:

Shoes and socks are the best thing. We can't have you wandering about bare foot.

RONNIE:

What about my tonsils?

DOCTOR:

No, shoes and socks are no good for tonsils. Come back and see me in six months.

RONNIE:

Right, doctor. Thank you very much, doctor.

DOCTOR:

Goodbye now Mr. Smith-Doctor. Oh, and don't forget your trousers. No good you wandering about like that. Surest way to catch tonsillitis.

Here is a sketch written for lugubrious comedian Les Dawson which is an example of the Reverse Sketch. Les set the sketch up with an opening monologue, thus:

MOST MEDIOCRE SHOW AWARD.

(Played by Les Dawson with intro.)

LES;

Well here we are again with another series. It's thanks to you viewers that wrote in with your comments that we've been brought back by public…transport. This is the first show of this new series and I am assured by the TV Company that they will spare nothing for your entertainment. And that's absolutely true. I asked what they can spare and they said "nothing." No, actually they're not that stingy. As a matter of fact when they wanted to announce this show they threw a press conference and a party in the fabulous Elizabethan Room of…Moe's Café. The Head of Light Entertainment was there. Nice fellow. As soon as he saw me he rushed over, took me aside… and left me there. Later he talked to me about the script. He said we have to be careful what we show because Mary Whitehouse is watching. I had to laugh. I mean, how can he complain about showing too much naked flesh with HIS bald head? Anyway, he insists we have a show that would be absolutely suitable for his own family. And this *will* be. We've cut out the clean parts. Anyway, it's about time we got into the show proper, and it may seem rather immodest, but we'd like to start off by acknowledging an award we received for the last series. Here it is…

WE SEE A MINIATURE SILVER OSCAR ON A PLINTH. IT'S A BIT DIFFERENT FROM THE HOLLYWOOD OSCAR IN THAT ITS RIGHT HAND IS UP WITH A THUMB TO ITS NOSE.

Yes, that's all ours. The Television Academy Award for The Most Mediocre Show Of The year. As you can see, it's solid plastic. And, choked up as I am with emotion, I think it's incumbent upon me to give praise to the other people without whom the series would never have sustained its high standard of mediocrity. Firstly, let's have out here the man who produced the show …Fernan Ficklewick.

TALL, SKINNY ODD-LOOKING BRETTON WOODS COMES OUT AND TAKES A BOW.

Fernan, we honestly couldn't have done it without you. It was your lack of decision in times of crisis that really clinched this award for us. Would you like to make a little speech?

BRETTON:

(STUTTERING) Well I…I…I…don't kn..know.

LES:

Beautifully put! Now you'd better go backstage and lie down. The undertaker wants to take your measurements.

BRETTON STARTS TO EXIT. THE AUDIENCE APPLAUD.

BRETTON:

(STUTTERING) Th…tha…thank…..

LES:

(GETTING RID OF HIM) Alright, I'll tell them for you. Mustn't overstrain yourself.

BRETTON WAVES A THANK YOU AND GOES.

LES:

There he goes. The only man I know who looks like his passport photo. Now the second man I want you to meet is our Floor Manager,

Percy Penfold, whose job it is to cue the entrance of everybody that comes on the show.

ROY BARRACLOUGH COMES ON WEARING EARPHONES AND CARRYING A CLIPBOARD. HE BOWS SHYLY.

LES:

Percy, you did a job that was, one can say in complete sincerity – absolutely lousy.

ROY:

(MODEST) Oh, it was nothing.

LES:

(FULL OF ADMIRATION FOR HIS MODESTY) "Nothing", he says! Why, if Percy here had given one cue on time…just one in a whole series…we'd never have got this award. He has a fine reputation, this lad. He's the only man I know who's guaranteed to give a "Five-minutes-to-opening" call six minutes after the show has finished. Tell them what you did to Bet Lynch on *Coronation Street*.

ROY:

(PROUDLY) I called her so late she wound up pulling pints for Lorraine Kelly on *The Breakfast Show*.

LES:

Thank you Percy Penfold.

APPLAUSE AS ROY EXITS.

LES:

Any youngsters viewing tonight that want to follow in Percy's footsteps can do the same as he did. Train ten years with Royal Mail. And now let us not forget the female side. The ladies that worked so tirelessly to keep us away from the path of true entertainment. The one lady in particular that I have in mind is our Script Girl, Lavinia Lonesome.

DAMARIS HAYMAN COMES OUT STRIDING HORSILY WITH SCRIPT IN HAND.

LES:

(TAKING SCRIPT FROM HER) Let me read to you one of the more memorable passages she typed from a sketch we did about the excessive amount of crime, passion, violence and political bias in Noddy in Toyland. (READS FROM SCRIPT) "Noody goose throt the dour onti the mean hale where everybondy is wanting fear ham." (to Damaris) And you did that all by yourself, didn't you?

DAMARIS:

Of curse oo dad!

LES:

Thank you Lavinia. Unfortunately she won't be with us next week as she will be down at The Old Bailey sitting on a jerry. Unfortunately there isn't time to thank everybody else individually, but I ought to mention our cameraman Anthony Hamstrung Jones…..

CUT TO CAMERAMAN LOOKING INTO HIS CAMERA. HE IS WEARING A PAIR OF BLUE TINTED MOTOR CYCLIST'S GOGGLES.

LES:

(CONTINUING)….who needs the eyeshade because he's only used to making blue movies. I'd also like to mention our Tea Girl, Mortitia the Yuppy. We call her a Yuppy because when any fellow asked to sleep with her she says "Yup!"

CUT TO BETTY AS SEXY TEA GIRL. SHE WINKS TO CAMERA.

And finally I must give due praise to our extinguished Director, Archibald Thickhead, a man whose lack of talent is only matched by his lack of taste.

CUT TO SHOW A MOUSTACHIOED, MIDDLE-AGED, ROMEO-TYPE.)

He always knows what he's after and never fails to get it.

WE SEE THE DIRECTOR LOOKING IN THE DIRECTION OF THE SEXILY CLAD TEA GIRL. HE WALKS PAST HER AND INTO THE OPEN ARMS OF THE MIDDLE AGED FRUMPY DAMARIS. THEY EMBRACE.

LES:

So, on behalf of all the people I've mentioned, plus our tone deaf Musical Orchestra Conductor, the old age pensioners we call our scriptwriters and myself....I'd like to say to The Television Academy that named us The Most Mediocre Show Of The Year...just this!

LES TURNS THE MINIATURE OSCAR STATUE SO THAT THE THUMBED NOSE IS POINTED AT CAMERA.

Several things for you to keep in mind. First is that the comedian (star of the show) gets the final laugh in the sketch. Second is to consider the cost. Building scenery is expensive, so try to keep the action in one set, or two at the most. Keep the cast down to just as many actors as are necessary. A cleverly worded one-sided phone call will let the audience know what the person at the other end is saying, without needing to actually have an actor at that other end.

Consider who your audience is going to be. If you are writing the sketch for a foreign market be aware of their sensibilities. Sex on TV is taboo in many countries where even kissing in public is considered to be a crime. A predominantly Catholic country would, quite naturally, object to the Dave Allen type jokes and sketches ridiculing the Pope. The Germans lost the last two Great Wars and don't like to be reminded of their defeat.

Your exercise for this lesson is to supply the synopsis for at least two sketches and an actual script for a sketch of your own choice.

LESSON FOUR – Writing Humorous Magazine Articles.

There's a huge dearth of writers who can fill the wishes of magazine editors desperate to find comedy to offer light entertainment for their readers. Bill Bryson, Jilly Cooper, Art Buchwald and Erma Bombeck have been the leading names in this field. All have written books which are fine examples of how to inject humour into an otherwise-serious topic.

Older folk, me included, often find the complexities of modern technology hard to understand. I am useless with computers. I see the curser as being me when the darn thing goes wrong. With this in mind, I poured my thoughts onto paper and penned this article.

MY BIGGEST COMPUTER ERROR WAS BUYING ONE.

Whoever said wisdom comes with age never considered me and computers. I have to confess to being computer illiterate. Those machines terrify me. Their keyboards seem to have more buttons than a Pearly Queen. And like my wife, they have a mind of their own, usually doing the opposite to what I want.

Trouble is I was born in the 1930's B.B.G., before Bill Gates. I'm too old to attune to the speed of modern technological invention where equipment is often outdated before you even get it out of the box.

It's for too-late developers like me that the manufacturers provide that "HELP" button. But I need further help to explain what it tells me. It assumes I already know more than I do. I'm baffled by the language it uses. The words are familiar to me, but in a totally different context.

I always thought a floppy disc was a record left too near a radiator. A RAM was a nanny goat's mate. Spam was something I was forced to eat during the war followed by tapioca pudding. Software was the Cashmere sweater I got for Christmas. A Hard Drive was that ride I took last Sunday on the M25. Scroll was something found in the Dead Sea. And eBay is a Northern expression ensued by the word "gum."

My granddaughter's only seven and already knows computer-speak. Yesterday she told me "I'm never going to have babies. They take nine months to download."

The salesman said my computer had a million uses. He didn't say the main one would be to keep the repair man busy. According to him my machine's had every virus known to man. And a few I'm sure he invented himself just to keep the money flowing from my bank account to his.

"This machine's best feature", the salesman gushed, "is its fantastic memory." He praised it so highly I was convinced it could even go back to a previous life. According to him it can store things in its memory for years. It's like my wife. She does just that and then brings them all back in one huge argument. Since I bought the darn thing Valerie hasn't stopped complaining. She says I spend so much time at the computer the only way we can communicate these days is by e-mail. She too is put off by computerization. We cancelled our Spanish holiday after she read that aircraft instruments are computerized. She's scared that if the computer crashes the plane will too.

Banks, incidentally, have even more trouble than I do. Every time I have a query they say "Sorry, can't deal with it now. Our computer is down." Funny how their computers are always down and their charges are always up. Light heartedly I answer "Your computer's down again? Does that mean you haven't had a byte all day?" They never laugh at my winsome wit and I now know why. The voice I heard was just a computerized answering machine. And even that's had more crashes than a Hollywood stunt man.

My friends who used to ring me for a chat now just send e-mails. Just think, if Alexander Graham Bell had known about e-mails he could have saved all that trouble inventing the telephone.

I get jokes sent to me by the score. And bargain offers of Viagra, cheap mortgages, low cost air flights and an irresistible dating service that promises to take my wife in part exchange.

The plain truth is that we wrinklies hate change. We'd prefer the status to stay quo. We fought a losing battle against all-figure telephone numbers, decimal currency and post codes. And when so-called action films dropped swashbuckling in favour of unbuckling, we had to reluctantly accept the porn is mightier than the sword. Our narrow minds were forced to broaden along with our hips and waistlines.

We can't control progress, but with the growth of computerization it seems to be controlling us. So Valerie and I have decided to capitulate and go the whole hog. Tomorrow we're buying a lap top and remembering that whereas a lap top was something our grandchildren sat on, now it is something they can show us how to work.

If you take the trouble to re-read the article you'll see how it was written. I started by listing every aspect I could think of connected with computers. My list included keyboard buttons... the "Help" button... Bill Gates... computer speak... floppy disc... RAM... Spam... software... hard drive... scroll... eBay... download... virus... and computer repairs... memory... email... computer being down... computer crashing... byte... jokes sent by e-mail... adverts for dating services... laptops.

There were other things on my list which I didn't use including URL... domain names... passwords... XP... Windows... attachments... internet... surfing... websites.

I stuck with the words that offered the best chance for a laugh, or at least a smile of recognition from fellow sufferers.

That article was immediately snapped up by *Writers' Forum* who then commissioned several more. My second article for them was inspired by a comment from comedy writer Johnny Speight about his early beginnings. He said he had a complete wall full of rejections before he made his first sale. I saw that as the basis for an article written in what's known as the "Reverse Angle." Read the following piece and you'll see what I mean.

BRAD ASHTON INSISTS ON SUCCESS AT ALL COSTS

When I first got the inkling to be a professional writer I was told the secret to success was to overcome early failure and persevere. They said "Every writer worth his sort had his bathroom walls papered with rejection slips before he hit the big time." So that was my target. A daunting one because, at that time, I had quite a large bathroom.

Anyway, hungry for early recognition as a writer, I set off to get those walls covered as quickly as possible. I formulated a plan guaranteed to earn me all those rejections. I would write tat for *Tatler*, articles with silly angles for *Angler's Weekly*, insignificant stuff for *Big Issue*. I wrote so many stinkers most of them were reviewed in obituary columns. I produced enough turkeys to make Bernard Matthews green with envy.

Those short, invective-filled, terse notes from editors were coming in thick and fast from every newspaper and magazine I submitted to. I was doing so well I even applied to the *Guinness Book of Records* to be the writer with the most rejections, but they rejected me. It's there for all to see, just above the hot tap that turns on my shower.

Shower is an appropriate term, because it is not only part of my plumbing, but also describes what many editors thought of my work. I even got rejection slips for articles sent in by other writers. They were so bad the editors assumed I'd written them.

As soon as one wall was full I threw a party to celebrate. Just a small party. I was determined not to let failure go to my head.

During that period I did take writing lessons and was advised by my teacher never to underestimate my talent. I mentioned this in a note to one editor whose swift reply was "You *couldn't* underestimate your talent!" I kept with the school for a whole month, during which they instilled in me enough confidence to write a concise, clear-cut, professional-looking letter, asking for my money back.

In addition to rejection slips, my mailbag was averaging four begging letters per day. All from editors begging me to stop writing. Mercilessly I carried on, determined to reach my goal.

While I was contemplating my novel and wondering how many rejection slips Shakespeare got before he became famous and whether Anne Hathaway objected to his bathroom décor, I encountered an unforeseen hurdle. Editors were recognizing my name on the back of the envelopes and saved their precious time by not even opening them. Being binned was a bind, a problem that had to be circumnavigated. I used pseudonyms.

At one time I wrote as a policeman, P.C. Wodehouse, then Raol Doll, William Forkner, Tennis E. Williams, Sigmund Fraud and even Ian Phlegming. For six weeks I changed my name more often than my socks. It worked. Those eagerly-awaited rejection slips came flooding in again. There was just one small sodden spot on my bathroom wall yet to be hidden. As the Bard himself might have said, I had to wipe "Out damn spot!"

My final rejection slip came from *The Investor's Chronicle* claiming my piece on the merits of investing in Enron were incredibly misguided. Bliss! I had achieved my target. I'd got through the initiation ceremony, as it were, so the rest should be easy. I could now be a successful writer. All I had to do was successfully write.

I announced to the world that I would be the next big comedy writer. After all, what had Carla Lane got that I hadn't? No, perhaps that wasn't a good choice. What had John Sullivan or Simon Nye or Ben Elton or Richard Curtis got that I hadn't? I mean, apart from talent.

Was the great literary world ready for me? All I needed was encouragement. It certainly didn't come from my Dad who thought I ought to do a "proper" job. He said he'd read somewhere there are only seven basic jokes "And they've all been used."

"So what?" I said, "I'll use them again and again in different disguises like most comedy writers do." That's my modus operandi and if the TV producers don't like my scripts they can just send them back to Don L. Duck, Shirl E. Temple, Wood E. Allen, Mike L. Grade, Orse N. Welles or any of the other aliases I choose to hide behind. And why not? If you write comedy like I do, wouldn't you?

That article was not only written in the reverse angle form, it was also self deprecating. I was making fun of myself rather than targeting someone else who might take umbrage and sue me and the magazine. Editors are wary about litigation and will reject any submissions that can involve them in a case of libel or slander.

There are many other causes for rejection of your work even if the editor acknowledges it would amuse his readers. Here's one I had rejected. See if you can figure out why.

IS IT A SIN TO BE CYNICAL?

When someone opens a sentence with "To be honest" to be honest, I don't believe them. I think it stems from my first visit to the dentist who said "This won't hurt a bit" – I don't know which bit he was referring to, but the rest of me hurt like mad.

As a fully paid-up sceptic, I have an inherent distrust of TV commercials. For instance, I don't believe advertised products that say they contain "less fat" or "less salt" – less than what?

The butter mountain in Russia? Or the salt mines in Siberia? I don't believe adverts for hotels in the Costa Brava that appear to offer a lot: could be when you get there it's just an empty lot.

I don't believe cheap package holiday bargains that make no mention of hidden extras. A friend of mine took one to New York – on the way back at Heathrow he was asked if he had anything to declare. He said "Yes, bankruptcy!"

I don't believe those loan companies who blatantly claim you can borrow yourself out of debt. Or the medical insurance schemes where you pay a fortune so you can have a free operation. I don't believe mobile phone companies that promise free calls but don't say they'll be from their salesmen pushing more expensive deals.

I don't believe those adverts for costly beauty products which say many women benefited from the results. What they don't mention is the women who benefited most were Helena Rubinstein, Elizabeth Arden and Estee Lauder. I'm suspicious of cheap sales of branded shampoos that could well be sham and smell like poo. Possibly the same firm that offers more dyes than you'll find in a Welsh phone directory.

I don't believe those "limited" half price furniture sales; they have more extensions than Gloria Beckham's hair. They urge you to "Buy now while stocks last!" I can confidently assure you that, in most cases, stocks will last as long as there's someone out there with money to buy them.

I don't believe adverts where banks compete with each other for efficiency. My bank, for instance, can't count properly, otherwise why would they have six windows and only two tellers?

I don't believe airlines who say they're making substantial cuts in fares without saying leg room too. Or roadside car repair services that say in the case of a breakdown all you have to do is phone them and wait. Last time I waited so long that by the time they came my car was almost obsolete.

As you can see, unlike the Monkees I am NOT a believer – probably because I have been so gullible in the past. I should never have believed the used car salesman who said the car he sold me would do 35 miles to the gallon. It turned out to be oil. Or the fast food café that said if I bought a whole meal I would get lots of chips. And there *were* lots of chips...in the crockery.

I used to buy packets of breaded fish until they reduced the content. Last time I bought one the fish inside was so small I was legally obliged to throw it back. I once bought an electronically operated garage door that kept my car securely locked in my garage – and me too when there was a power cut.

To be honest (did I really say that?) I preferred those TV adverts in olden days when commercial breaks were very much shorter. Today they're never-ending. On television now it takes longer to watch an old film than it took to make it in the first place.

I used to love those old slogans like "Put a tiger in your tank". That's still not such a bad idea. It would be cheaper than what we're now paying for petrol. And there was "Go to work on an egg." That was pre-Edwina Currie and her threat of Salmonella.

"I wonder where the yellow went" was for toothpaste that whitened teeth and protected gums. I even remember the joke I used at the time about not buying it because I was trying to transcend dental medication.

And what happened to that little French girl advertising yoghurt who was a "Right little madam."? That was over 20 years ago. Who knows, by now she could be a BIG madam working in a Parisian bordello.

I have to admit I was never convinced by those talking chimps lovingly extolling the virtues of PG Tips. I'm sure it was a con; chimps can't talk, and if you meet one who tells you he can, he's probably lying.

I'm afraid it's a fact of life that TV will always be with us; that's why we should all keep telling our children fairy stories to prepare them for the commercials.

You've probably realised by now that the article you've just read, was suggesting a lot of advertising could be dodgy. Magazines rely on adverts for their living, so publishing my send-up of advertisers would be counter productive. I foolishly wasted my time writing it in the first place.

I've found the easiest-to-sell articles are based on things I have personally experienced. For thirty six years my wife was a Yoga teacher. Yoga is extremely popular today, especially among women. So I aimed for The Women's Page of the Daily Express with this article.

BRAD ASHTON LOOKS AT THE FUNNY SIDE OF YOGA

Yoga has become the bane of my life? That foolhardy fad just won't fade. It's kept more women occupied than Warren Beatty, Hugh Hefner and John Prescott all together?

Originally exported to us from India, Yoga's their revenge for years of oppression under the British Raj. I suspect it was invented by an Untouchable who was probably touched at the time.

Among the U.K.'s fairer sex it's spread like strawberry jam at a cream tea party. Women who previously whispered behind closed doors about each other, are now unashamedly gossiping about Yoga. "Guess who was seen with who in what position!"

Yoga is supposed to be all about breathing and stretching. What it stretches most is my credulity. My first encounter was watching it being demonstrated by a narrow-hipped Indian gentleman dressed in nothing but an oversized nappy. A sort of Ghandi Man. I remember thinking he's so thin he'd need to stand in the same place twice to cast a shadow...

My wife Valerie was so smitten she not only took up Yoga, but became a teacher of the art and now conducts six 2-hour sessions a week. As a Yoga-widower-cum-author I'm left to sit at home just contemplating my novel. We have a perfect understanding. I never go to her classes and she doesn't laugh at my jokes.

To be honest, I did peep into one of her classes at the beginning and what I saw still feeds my nightmares. An assortment of 30 female bodies were strewn around the floor like an Amazon battlefield. All torturing their tendons, bullying their biceps and masochistically mutilating their muscles in a yearn for the burn.

One woman had the soles of her feet perched on the back of her head while another had her legs crossed upwards so her toes supported her chin. A third had her left hand over her right shoulder trying to shake hands with herself behind her own back. Yet another lady, in a peculiar inverted position was staring straight up my trouser leg. All were in double-jointed, painful positions. Well, painful to look at anyway. The only way I would try them is if I was filleted first.

Some women suffer Yoga in the mistaken belief it will trim their bulging waistlines, or hive the odd ton off their unsightly love handles. It doesn't. But it does give them a twenty minute afternoon kip with the excuse that they're meditating in their personal mantra. For those that don't know, mantra is a phrase or word you repeat to yourself for the whole twenty minutes till it's instilled in your brain. And the word I've been trying to get Valerie to choose as a mantra is "divorce".

In addition to the 84 different positions in Yoga, there are also different types. The two most popular are Ashtanga and Hatha. If Shakespeare were still around I'm sure he would have chosen the Hatha-way. Yes, you're right; my own mantra should be "Avoid such terrible puns."

Getting back to my spouse, Valerie's six Yoga sessions a week make her fit for anything, except to live with. Her stress relief exercises have taken the tension out of her body, and put them into our marriage. It's fast becoming impossible to see eye to eye with a wife that spends so much time standing on her head. She's a fanatic. I suspect she even sits on the loo in the Lotus position.

It would be easier if she just kept the Yoga side of her life to herself, but no. She's determined to get me involved, vowing to make me healthier even if it kills me. In our house I'm forbidden to slouch on the couch or lounge in the lounge. If caught I am severely reprimanded and subjected to a lecture on proper posture followed by a series of back-straightening exercises which, while increasing my height, rapidly decreases my will to live.

A typical day starts with Valerie's deep breathing exercises. So deep, every intake turns the room into a vacuum. The main problem is she has no sense of humour where Yoga is concerned. And that's not funny. If she knew I was writing this, I'd be on bread and water for a week. Mind you, that would be a lot better than the food she serves me up now. Yoga-followers are strict vegetarians. Meat in our house is as scarce as a national health dentist.

The Ashton daily menu consists of grilled grapes, hazelnut hash and roasted radish. It's stuffed so full of vitamins there's no room left for any taste. Even our cat with its 9 lives to risk has taken to eating out.

Our bookshelves are crammed full with reading material on you-know-what. I've read *Yoga For Health... Yoga For Beauty... Yoga For Pregnancy* - I still haven't mastered that one... *Yoga For The Young... Yoga For The Old... Yoga For Those That Are Old But Lie About Their Age... Yoga For Backache... Yoga For Frontache... Yoga For Earache.* There's even one called *Yoga For Sex*, but the exercises are so tiring I've re-titled it *Yoga OR Sex.*

It's almost a decade since my better half became so wholeheartedly addicted to Yoga and I have now decided that for the sake of peace and matrimonial harmony, as I can't beat her I may as well join her. So let me just get into position and sign off...

Pass me a soya cutlet, would you?
Ah, that's better! You know, this doesn't feel so bad after all.

The Daily Express Women's Page Editor not only bought it, but took me to lunch to commission a series on the humorous side of my relationships with my wife and three children.

The very next day I received an enormous phone bill incurred mostly by my wife who I now refer to as my chattering chattel. I was angry, so in order to swallow the pill of the bill, I sat down determined to find a funny side to it. Here's how it appeared in The Daily Express.

EVER HAD AN OBSCENE PHONE BILL?

My wife is a phonoholic. She's never off the phone. Valerie's hang-up is she can't hang up. She even chats for half an hour to a wrong number. The only thing longer than her conversations is the phone bill itself. The last bill was four pounds. Not money, weight! It was like a book. It had more pages than War and Peace.

It started way back when BT had that slogan "Someone somewhere is waiting to hear from you." She phoned halfway round the world trying to find out who it was. Among the calls listed on the bill were to her Aunt Sally in San Francisco, her Uncle Jack in Johannesburg, her Cousin Sidney in Adelaide and even her Cousin Adelaide in Sidney. She rings everybody. If it were possible, she'd even give Alexander Graham a bell.

We must be the only household in London whose phone still has a finger dial. That's because she's never off it long enough to put a new one in. It's no joke. We've even had to put an extension out in the garden so she can occasionally get some fresh air.

This problem is quite common. There are many hungry husbands who come home from work to find the only thing warm in the house is the phone. One fellow sufferer told me his wife regularly sneaks out of bed at 2 a.m. to have a long conversation with the speaking clock. Another said he came down to breakfast and found his wife on both extensions at the same time talking to herself.

Phone-ins on radio are besieged by these poor women desperate to speak to someone. They even use aliases to be put through more times. My wife's used every name from Ada Ackerman to Zelda Zukosky. She's spoken to Wogan more times than his own Missus. Once, for a week she couldn't speak because she had laryngitis. BT sent her a Get Well Soon card every day.

Valerie now uses a cordless phone as a safety measure. She knows that if there was a cord I'd probably strangle her with it. While she's using Orange, I'm turning purple. It's been going on for years. It seems since we were engaged she's been engaged.

Most recognisable number on the phone bill is Valerie's mother. She calls her for about three hours every day. And her house is only in the next street. Our kids don't know that. They think Grandma lives in the phone. I asked her, "What on earth do you find to talk about for three hours?" She said, "We talk about how mean you are." I gave Valerie strict instructions to tell her mother that I, the mean one, insists future calls must be no longer than three minutes. So she told her mother that she'll set the egg timer and when that runs out she'll put the phone down. I was happy until she added, "Then you can call me back and reverse the charges."

At one time I thought of having the phone cut off. But it wouldn't have helped. Women get cunning in desperate circumstances. She'd probably knock off a policeman's hat to get arrested and have that one obligatory phone call. In the world of communications my Valerie's quite famous. In fact I think Talk Talk was named after her.

Finally, together with a group of other similarly sad spouses I have formed a new organisation called *Phonoholics Anonymous*. When the problem gets really acute the husband calls us and we send over a Trappist Monk to impose a vow of silence.

I bet when Valerie reads this, she'll phone in to complain.

I've said earlier that most of the best ideas for articles come from your own experiences. None of us has gone through life without finding ourselves in an embarrassing situation. Writing about *My Most Embarrassing Moments* would make a good article. Or after a holiday to, say, India or China *Not Only Did I See Poverty, I Brought It Back With Me,* telling of all the unexpected expenses you faced on that holiday. Or *The Shock Of Hiring An Electrician* telling of how he was called in to fix a faulty switch and convinced you the whole house needed re-wiring. Or *Buy Cheap and You Get More Than You Bargained For,* about the hidden costs in buying a house or car or whatever.

Or *I Was Almost One of the Chosen People* about the time you were roped into taking part in a police identity parade because you closely resembled the suspected criminal. Or *I Sat Down To Stand Up For My Rights* about the day you refused to leave a store until the manager was called to hear your complaint.

All those suggestions have one thing in common; intriguing titles that make the reader want to know more. They will also engage the attention of the editor and get you over that first hurdle.

I have covered the Reverse Angle article, but very similar is the Negative article. It's also known as the How Not To Theme. After enough research has made you an expert on the subject you'll be able to write *How Not To Be A Successful Gambler* or *How Not To Be A Successful Investor* or *How Not To Be A Successful Salesman* or *How Not To Be A Successful Spouse.*

If you are looking for a subject and your mind goes blank, do what a lot of professionals find extremely useful. They rifle through old magazines and select subjects they can put their own individual slant on. In no way am I suggesting plagiarism. What I'm saying is that you will be finding subjects and themes you hadn't previously thought of and that open your mind to their possibilities for your next article.

I read an article by a lady named Sylvia Porter in a *Chicago Tribune* edition of 1953. It was about Confidence Tricks. I was so impressed I hungrily searched through other magazines and books until I became an expert on the subject. I built up a file containing details of 400 different scams. It led to my writing a regular syndicated column called *Spot The Con* which ran for 114 consecutive weeks in 23 provincial papers. That, in turn, got me commissioned by BBC radio to write 60 half hour shows called *Pro's & Cons* exposing three confidence tricks per show.

It taught me the value of taking the time and trouble to study a subject enough to be acknowledged as a leading expert on it. I would advise you to do the same. Pick your own subject that you'll enjoy researching. Though I did all my researching free at the British Museum Library, which has over 13,000,000 books, magazines and newspapers, much of that same information is now available on computer search engines.

One question I'm always being asked by would-be writers is "How can I be sure my ideas will not be stolen?" My answer to that is that if you are worried about your ideas being purloined you've given yourself the perfect excuse not to bother to write in the first place. Ideas alone cannot be copyrighted anyway. An idea is not a property as such. A finished article *is* a property, and can be protected by copyright. Though not actually foolproof, the simplest way to prove you wrote an article is to post a copy of it to yourself and leave it unopened. In the unlikely event of a court case you can then prove you wrote the property before the date registered on the envelope.

I do however, urge you not to worry about your hard work being stolen. That's the very furthest thing from an editor's mind. If you have written something he thinks is good, he'll do his utmost to encourage you to write more. Editors love to discover new talent and you could be the next big discovery.

Here are a few final guidelines you might find helpful:

Before submitting anything to a magazine, make sure you have read at least two back issues to see the length, style and themes of the articles they've selected to publish.

Avoid overlong paragraphs. Try to keep them to a maximum of eight lines.

Avoid using too many clichés as this shows lack of originality.

It is OK to use quotes as long as you state clearly who said or wrote them.

Don't expect everything you write to be perfect straight away. As American playwright Moss Hart said, "Good plays aren't written, they're re-written." If you're not facing a deadline, sleep on your work overnight and look at it the next day to see if re-writes might make it sharper.

Include pictures if you can. They not only attract the eye of the reader, but authenticate your story.

Your local public library should have copies of *Benn's Press Directory* and *Willing's Press Guide* in their reference section. Both these publications list details of every newspaper and magazine published in the U.K. and around the world. They will tell you the subject, circulation and actually name the editorial staff so you can submit your article to a person rather than just "The Editor" of your chosen magazine.

Your exercise for Lesson Four is to write a 750 word humorous piece and suggest a magazine you think it would be suitable for.

LESSON FIVE: Characters And Relationships For Sitcoms.

The main reason we watch situation comedies is because we like the principal characters and are interested in what happens to them. We may not always sympathise, but we do empathise with them. They become like members of our own family. To some people they are real, which is the essence of their success. We care about them and can identify with their problems. Jack Benny accredited his popularity as the world's most parsimonious man to the fact that "Everyone in my audience knows someone like me."

The characters we create do not have to be nice people. They can be selfish, uncaring and rude like Basil Fawlty in *Fawlty Towers* or Alf Garnett in *Till Death Us Do Part*.

But even those two men needed to have their vulnerable side in order to make them acceptable to the audience. Basil Fawlty was afraid of his wife. Alf Garnett could never get his wife to take him seriously. That was part of their vulnerability.

It's advisable to know who your audience are likely to be so you can avoid offending them. A well known pair of comedy writers were banned from working for London Weekend TV because they wrote about a homosexual in a way that offended the then Head of Light Entertainment who was himself gay. I wrote several hundred shows for German television, but like Basil Fawlty I "never mentioned the war" because they lost the last two and can be very sensitive about it.

Spike Milligan wrote a series called *The Melting Pot* in which he used derogatory jokes about many nationalities, races, creeds and religions. If he left out insulting a minority group it wasn't intentional. Spike's reasoning was that as long as you made fun of everybody, nobody could take offence. The BBC didn't agree and though the series was made, it was never shown on TV. Also languishing in the archives are six scripts written by Johnny Speight for the proposed second, follow-on series of *Curry & Chips* which centred on the antics of a "shifty" Asian landlord. Apparently the first series caused so many complaints the second was never made. Political correctness can be a huge constraint, but it affords TV companies a good reason to reject a writer's work if he crosses the line, no matter how funny the script may be.

Statistics show that, apart from sport, wives usually make the decision which shows to watch. Whilst most women like weepie and romantic shows, men go more for action thrillers. A good writer will attempt to combine as many facets as possible in his comedy. Intrigue, romance, action and pathos are good ones to start with. In a later lesson I'll deal with storylines and show how this is done.

This lesson pinpoints character and I think we can learn a lot from the past. Perhaps the most popular comedians down through the ages have been Laurel & Hardy, Charlie Chaplin, Buster Keaton, Tony Hancock and even Norman Wisdom. The common denominator, the one thing they all relied on aside from laughs, was pathos. They scored best when faced with adversity. Their writers deliberately put in scenes that made us feel sorry for the comedians. Pathos, cleverly and sparsely inserted in a script will draw in a bigger audience. Pathos equals vulnerability. Even Phil Silvers as the egocentric, pushy Sergeant Bilko had moments of sadness when his long-time girlfriend kept rejecting him. Vulnerability rounds out characters. It makes them more human.

Your characters should never be black and white. They should have a reason for their actions and always be liable to change if their circumstances changed. But at the end of an episode they should be back as they started. You can never be sure which order the episodes will be shown on TV, which is why the principal characters must remain constant.

Alf Garnett, TV's archetypal bigot, believed he was a true patriot because he hated foreigners and minority groups. If you dig deeper into his character you'll find that he didn't really hate them so much as fear them. He was motivated by fear. Writer Johnny Speight based Garnett on his own father who claimed to loathe Blacks, Asians, Catholics, Jews, Muslims, just about anybody who wasn't, in his opinion, true British. He was a stevedore and ruthless militant against what he called "Them foreign gits who come over here to take our jobs away!"

In *Dad's Army* Arthur Lowe starred as self-appointed Captain Mainwaring, a pompous ass who took on the job of commanding a war time platoon of civilian soldiers in Britain's Home Guard. He was a class conscious snob who firmly believed that being a bank manager he outranked the butchers, bakers, postmen, etc. that made up his motley crew of weary warriors. We Brits love to see pomposity punctured and that was the basis for every episode that David Croft and Jimmy Perry wrote.

Tony Hancock's main characteristic was frustration. He felt the world was conspiring to keep him an underdog. He longed to rise from pleb to celeb. Tony had delusions of grandeur and got angry when nobody else acknowledged his worth. He had a continual battle with officialdom and saw himself as the saviour of the downtrodden, vainly fighting their lost causes. Even his liaisons with the fair sex were frustrating. He always fancied women that didn't fancy him.

Frank Spencer, as so brilliantly portrayed by Michael Crawford, was a loser. A nebbish type who tried so hard to reach the height of being average. He was gawky, clumsy and naïve. His poor dress sense alone set him down two points on the social scale. Like Peter Falk's Columbo, Frank's soiled raincoat was so famous it probably could have toured on its own. Frank was one of those people pitfalls were made for. All writer Raymond Allen had to do was to find manholes for him to drop into, banana skins to slip on and ledges to fall off. His vulnerability was in being disastrously honest and innocently accepting, without question, anything that came his way.

Psychiatrists insist that we laugh loudest at the lower classes out of relief that we are more fortunate than they are. Alf Garnett, Harold and Albert Steptoe and Frank Spencer, prison inmate Norman Stanley Fletcher and failed con-man Del Boy Trotter, all being working class, go a long way to proving that point.

But the characters in *To The Manor Born, Jeeves & Wooster* and *Never The Twain* prove that poverty and humble surroundings are not the only ingredients for successful sitcoms. The essential criterion is that your characters are believable in their reactions to the situations you create for them. Another extremely important factor is that they stand out because they are different from the people around them. The word to remember here is "contrast." Contrast highlights character traits.

In *Fawlty Towers* the frenetic Basil Fawlty contrasted with his business-like, cool headed, tactful wife Sybil; in *Steptoe & Son* ambitious Harold contrasted with his scheming father Albert; in *Porridge* cynical old lag Fletcher contrasted with young inexperienced cell-mate Godber; in *Open All Hours* canny, cheating Arkwright contrasted with his young unworldly, easily manipulated nephew Granville; in *Hancock* downtrodden Tony contrasted with happy-go-lucky Sid James who saw a silver lining in every cloud. They were so different they constantly clashed with each other thus providing the basis for useful storylines.

In the case of the *Steptoes, Porridge, Open All Hours* and *Only Fools And Horses* the generation gap played a great part too. It widened the prospective audience because two different generations were able to identify with the characters.

What writers aim for are believable reasons for their main characters to be confronted by something unexpected that throws them out of kilter; twists in the plot or encounters with other characters that have different opinions or agenda. For this they use what's known as the "pivotal" character(s). It could be one of the regular cast or an outsider brought in to upset the norm. In simple terms, the pivotal character acts as a sort of feed providing the conflict that fuels the situation and moves it along.

Songwriters are forever being asked which comes first, the music or words. In almost every case it's the music with the lyricist adding his contribution afterwards. With situation comedy very few writers create the situation before they invent the characters to inhabit it. Usually it is the other way around. They create the characters and then put them into situations that best exploit their potential for laughs. In short, the best sitcom series are character-led.

Creating a new character

How does one create a new character? Henrik Ibsen said he imagined going on a long railway journey and getting into conversation with his fellow passengers. He'd recollect their attitudes, body language and speech patterns. Then he would decide his opinions of them. That system worked for Ibsen. His contemporary Anton Chekhov used another approach. He thought that writers should know everything about their characters, their net worth, their shoe size, their medical history, etc. Chekhov insisted it didn't matter if none of this information was passed on to his audiences, what mattered was that he had the full perception of the character and was therefore able to produce a more rounded person.

Other writers keep a diary of all the new people they've met that day with a note of what made them different, or at least interesting. Some borrow characters from books they've read or plays they've seen and place them in a situation or environment of the writer's own choosing. We all have our own methods. Mine is to imagine I am a psychiatrist with the character I am trying to create, lying on my couch. I learn about them by asking questions, often very personal searching questions. Then I build a very comprehensive file based on their answers.

Before asking those questions I will decide for myself their physical side. Their age, sex, height, build, complexion, eye colour and hair colour. I ask myself whether they are good looking, dress smart or sloppily. I will need to know their marital status, national origin, sexuality, profession or trade, financial position and their ambitions.

Further searching inquisition will establish whether they are lower class, working class, middle or upper class. Are they professionals or tradesmen or unskilled? Are they happy at their work and with their lifestyle? Are they religious, agnostic or an atheist? Are they shy, gregarious, introvert or extrovert? What are their hobbies, vices or special interests? Who are their favourite authors? What are their political affiliations or views? Are they leaders or followers? Do they view the future with optimism or pessimism, or are they fatalists leaving it all to God?

I have given you enough questions to think about for the time being. The answers to every one of them will add colour to the character being created. It does not necessarily need to be a total creation from scratch. We know that Johnny Speight modelled Alf Garnett on his own racially-bigoted father and that John Cleese's template for Basil Fawlty was the owner of a hotel he once stayed at in Eastbourne. Perhaps you have an unusual relative, neighbour or colleague whose idiosyncrasies you could draw on as the basis for the lead in a new sitcom. Just remember that we are all different. Even identical twins have individual characteristics which dictate their reactions and attitudes to the same situations. Your target is to know each character so well that you can see the situation through their eyes.

Though it is useful to decide on your character's speech pattern, characterisation doesn't always require dialogue. The old axiom that actions speak louder than words certainly worked for Rowan Atkinson's *Mr. Bean* series. Eric Sykes's classic silent comedy *The Plank* was a masterful attempt at recapturing the kind of universal comedy Max Sennett filled cinemas with prior to the advent of Talkies. Mime is a powerful language understood all over the world and foreign repeats can seriously multiply your earnings.

We can learn a lot about people from how they act, where they go, what car they drive and what clothes they wear. Also from their hairstyles, the kind of house they live in and its furnishings. This brings me to the shortcut that telegraphs clues about a person before we've even seen him or her. Your script should feed as much information as possible to the set designers. Where a man lives or works says a lot about him. If he has a plush office, we already assume he is an executive. If merely a portioned-off cubicle, we know his job is more menial. Costume designers too can provide a good source of information. Have they dressed your character to look staid or flashy? If female, are her clothes fashionable, smart, pretty or deliberately revealing? Our clothes make statements about us that send out messages about the kind of person we are.

Probably the biggest enemy a sitcom writer has is time. I don't mean meeting a delivery deadline for a finished script, though that can be difficult enough. I'm referring to the task of having to squeeze a complete story, beginning middle and end, into what should be a half hour slot, but with commercial breaks and previews for other shows, is usually no more than just twenty two minutes. Even the BBC which has no commercials spends about four minutes of each half hour promoting its other forthcoming shows.

When a series is already up and running the writing is easier because your regular viewers are au fait with the characters and their environment. The hardest episode is the very first in which you introduce your people, their relationships, their home and/or workplace and their normal routine way of life. That's why any possible saving of time is worth chasing after. For instance, there may be a display of golf or athletic trophies, intellectual tomes on the bookshelves or even pop idol posters on bedroom walls that tell us about their owners.

The first time we meet a sitcom character we can see if they are normal or, in some way, different. If he is asleep in bed at night that is normal. If he is in bed during the day he might be ill, lazy, unemployed or a night worker. If he goes to work on a bus or train or drives a car, that is normal. But if he wears a smart suit and goes to work on a motorbike, he is different. If he eats in a restaurant with the serviette on his lap, he's normal. If it is tucked into the neck of his shirt, he is different. If he is reading a tabloid newspaper, he is probably working class. If it's *The Times* he is more likely to be a businessman and therefore upper class. These establishing features all save time.

The greatest and most practical time saver is in the hands of the writer. He has to avoid the mistake most new writers make of spending the first four or five pages establishing the characters before introducing the actual storyline for that episode. The professional and most efficient way is to commence the story on page one and have the viewers learn about the people by the way they react to the problems you've set them. Here's a brief example of what I mean:

INT.   DINING ROOM   MORNING.

GEORGE AND MARGARET, A MIDDLE AGED WORKING CLASS COUPLE, ARE SEATED AT THE BREAKFAST TABLE. THEY HAVE JUST FINISHED EATING AND ARE DRINKING THEIR COFFEE AS THEY READ. SHE IS READING THE TABLOID NEWSPAPER AND HE IS READING SOME PAPERS HE HAS JUST GOT OUT OF AN ENVELOPE.

MARGARET:

(INCREDULOUSLY) It says here that Petula Clark's only seventy. I can't believe that.

GEORGE:

If you think that's incredible, you should read this!

MARGARET:

What is it?

GEORGE:

Our phone bill. I think they've included the national debt.

MARGARET:

(GUILTILY) Is it a lot then?

GEORGE:

A lot? In monopoly I could buy the whole of Mayfair for less!

I see most of these calls are to your mother. At least six a day. What on earth do you find to talk about?

MARGARET:

What a stingy husband I've got!

In those few short speeches I have introduced the conflict. Margaret overspends and George is determined to put a stop to it. As the storyline evolves, he will demand she cuts back on phone calls and she, in return, will insist he gives up smoking. Both will suffer from withdrawal symptoms and become so irritable, cantankerous and difficult to live with that they finally settle on a truce and go back to the way they were before, deciding it's the lesser of two evils.

Whereas that conflict was over money, the same couple could have prolonged arguments over their bad driving habits, or who is the better cook, or even that green eyed monster - jealousy. A quick set-up for the jealousy option could start like this:

INT. LIVING ROOM. EVENING.

GEORGE AND MARGARET ARE SEATED SIDE BY SIDE ON THE COUCH. SHE IS FIDDLING WITH THE REMOTE CONTROL TRYING TO FIND SOMETHING DECENT TO WATCH ON TV. HE IS READING A NEWSPAPER.

MARGARET:

Not much to watch on TV tonight except *Casualty*.

GEORGE:

Carry on like that and you'll be on *Casualty* yourself with a sprained thumb. Put that thing down!

SHE RELUCTANTLY PUTS DOWN THE REMOTE CONTROL.

MARGARET:

Pity *The Antiques Road Show's* not on tonight. I love that Michael Aspel. He's real handsome.

GEORGE:

(DISPARAGINGLY) Handsome? Him? It's all make-up and lighting. I mean, take away that silver hair and fake tan and what have you got left?

MARGARET:

You!

GEORGE:

None of those blokes look the same off TV. Just take that Rodney Peabody who's all over the girls in that soap opera. There's a picture here of him at some charity do. He could play Dracula, without make-up.

MARGARET:

Well he's aged a bit. But he was a good-looker when I knew him.

GEORGE:

(SURPRISED) You knew Rodney Peabody? When did you know him?

MARGARET:

When he was plain Bert Higginbottom. He was in my class at school. Believe it or not, I had a crush on him for ages.

GEORGE:

(AMUSED) But he didn't fancy you?

MARGARET:

No. He had a crush on the teacher.

GEORGE:

Even then he was after the girls.

MARGARET:

It was a male teacher.

GEORGE:

(SURPRISED) He's gay?

MARGARET:

Very. Never went near us girls.

GEORGE:

I don't believe it. In his biography it says he's slept in as many beds as George Washington.

MARGARET:

Could be true if Washington was still in them.

GEORGE

No, I still can't believe it.

MARGARET:

Well I can easily check. That school re-union I've been invited to next week, he'll probably be there. I wasn't bothering to go, but I think I will now. You don't mind, do you?

GEORGE:

No, go if you want to, but there's one thing I still don't understand. You say you were in the same class at school, yet you're forty five and (REFERS TO NEWSPAPER) he says here he's only forty.

MARGARET:

He never was good at arithmetic.

To continue the story, all we need is someone to tell George that Rodney was cured of being gay years ago and is now he really is a womaniser and is only going to the school re-union to find more women to bed. This being a sitcom, the jealously possessive George would inveigle his way into the re-union party to keep a protective eye on Margaret and protect her from the famous lecher. He can either do this by pretending to have been in the class, which can lead to many laughs as he lies about his involvement in their reminiscences about their old schooldays, or get himself hired as a waiter at the party and shadow his wife to avoid her being in too close contact with Rodney.

With jealousy as the story's motivation George can do all sorts of outrageous things that embarrass Margaret and keep the comedy flowing. I guess the best ending would be discovering that Rodney really is gay after all and makes a play for George instead of Margaret.

Many writers use speech patterns to define a character. Ronnie Barker's stuttering in *Open All Hours* or Fulton McKay's speaking with a curled lip in *Porridge*, or Warren Mitchell's loud-mouth Cockney in *'Til Death Us Do Part*, Or John Cleese's clipped anger tones in *Fawlty Towers*. These traits are most often put in by the actors themselves, but the writer can suggest any such peculiarities if it helps make the character more distinctive.

Your exercise for this lesson is to describe any character you may have encountered in your daily life that struck you as odd or amusing and then write a speech for them that would best convey to the reader how you see that person.

LESSON SIX – Formulating Ideas For A Sitcom Series

The best ideas are undoubtedly based on truth. You start with something that has actually happened, or *can* actually happen, and exploit all its possibilities for humour. There are about fifty regular storylines that have been used, and perhaps over-used, in the past. The public, bless 'em, usually don't recognise the stories because the writers have been clever enough to switch the locations and inhabit them with their own characters. In other words, two different people might react in different ways to any given situation. A bank manager or dustman, a doctor or hypochondriac or even a man or woman.

I point that out to convince you there's no shame in using an already-worked plot line if you approach it from a different character's point of view or position. Imagine, if you would, *Porridge* where two convicts share a cell; just how much difference there would be if they were women. Or supposing the cellmates were a couple like Basil Fawlty and Spanish non-English-speaking waiter Manuel. You can pick your own assortment of odd characters locked together in that confined space and gauge their reactions to one another. The more opposite they are, the better opportunities they afford for comedy.

If you want to perpetuate the popular old joke you could have the inmates as a Scotsman, an Irishman and a Jew. But, if you do that, be careful not to exaggerate the usual perception of them and so become offensive.

The most important element of a sit com is "conflict". You need to set your lead character(s) a problem that needs to be solved. It could be someone else's problem that they get involved in and, in trying to help, create a bigger problem. It could be because they have misunderstood the problem or been fooled into getting the wrong angle on it.

If you have two main characters, usually a husband and wife, then the conflict could be confined to them. Perhaps they disagree on where to go on holiday, which school their children should go to, which car to buy, whether to allow a relative to stay with them (such as the wife's mother or father)...... I've even heard of couples arguing about whether to spend the money buying a joint burial plot. They could disagree on whether a prospective son-in-law is suitable for their daughter, or prospective daughter-in-law for their son.

When you have decided on a conflict you give thought to the possible ways of solving it. You'll be looking for a solution that has the possibility to backfire and cause further conflict. Then comes the difficult task of resolving the final problem to end the episode. Another choice of ending is to get the characters back to where they started. That's how we often ended the episodes of *Life With The Lyons* when I was working on that series.

If you're writing an ensemble show with a regular group of characters as in *Are You Being Served?*, *Hi-Di-Hi* or *Bread* the big problem is finding a plot that utilises all the characters. Some of those subsidiary characters will be so strong you must limit their part so they don't completely overshadow the stars of the show. Blakey in *On the Buses* was a prime example and used sparingly in each episode. Bluebottle in *The Goon Show* was so strong a character, writer Spike Milligan didn't bring him in till twelve minutes into an episode and his part ran for a maximum of two minutes. Kenneth Williams similarly so in the radio episodes of *Hancock*.

Jack Benny's writers had four or five characters that did just a cameo appearance in each episode. *Are You Being Served?* certainly regularly included a scene for Mr.Humphries to get in his catchphrase "I'm Free" and for Mrs Slocum to mention "My pussy." Catchphrases are a great asset, but very difficult to plan. They are usually discovered by accident because of the way an actor says what could have been planned as an innocuous line of dialogue.

Each writer, or pair of writers, has their own way of setting about writing a sit com. Eric Sykes, for instance divided his storyline into five roughly equal sections and wrote each part as though it were a sketch. Galton and Simpson said it took them two weeks to write a *Steptoe & Son* episode. The first four days were thinking-up and discarding storylines till they found one they were happy with. Then they'd spend a week writing about sixty pages of script and spend two days reducing it to the 28 pages it needed to be. The final day was spent honing and polishing it to get the perfect finished product.

Wolfe & Chesney used a different technique. Chesney would concoct the story line and Wolfe would fill in the funny dialogue. Much the same way a composer and lyricist would work.

My own method was to write the plot as a short story of about 1,000 words. That gave me the construction I needed, a beginning, middle and an end. Then I would keep expanding the short story by fleshing it out with the actual dialogue. When I reached the happy point where I had all the dialogue I needed, I would then type it out in script form.

It's a useful exercise to choose a situation and imagine, in your own mind, how Alf Garnett, Basil Fawlty, Delboy Trotter or even Tony Hancock would cope in those circumstances. That is the key to good sitcom writing. The writer creates a believable situation and then metamorphoses himself into being the character he inserts into it. That is the best and really the only way to keep the character consistent. But even consistency is not always necessary. The characters can change if, say, they are drunk or under hypnosis or have received a nasty bump on the head resulting in a "believable" (there's that word again), change.

The writer has to decide whether to start with his characters or his situation. Let us, for a moment, suppose he hit on the same idea as Ronnie Wolfe and Ronnie Chesney created for *The Rag Trade*. It was a small factory where the male boss was continually at loggerheads with the militant female shop steward who called a strike at every possible opportunity. Now picture the same set up with reversed roles. Make the boss a pretty woman and have a male shop steward on the lines of Peter Sellers in *I'm Alright Jack*.

Elaine Stritch and Donald Sinden starred as American employer and British butler in *Two's Company*. Then along came *To The Manor Born* which was originally written as an impoverished upper class widow who sold her mansion to an American and lived under the same roof as his tenant. Bernard Braden was actually nominated to play the American with Penelope Keith as the snobbish lady. Someone pointed out that the contrast was too much like Stritch & Sinden and chose Peter Bowles to play a Hungarian supermarket chain owner as the landlord instead. Because it was probably too difficult for Bowles to sustain a Hungarian accent and get laughs throughout the series, they recruited versatile actress Daphne Heard to handle the accent playing his immigrant mother.

Incidentally, *Two's Company* was tried out in The States with comedian Peter Cook in the Donald Sinden role, but had a very short run. It took the huge talent of Sinden to make the butler snobbish enough for the necessary contrast between him and his employer.

The right casting is crucial to the success of a sitcom series. It's hard to imagine anyone other than John Cleese as Basil Fawlty, Michael Crawford as Frank Spencer or Warren Mitchell as Alf Garnett. The BBC archives are full of sitcom pilots that were recorded but never broadcast because the lead character or their chemistry with the other characters stilted the comedy.

It was Galton & Simpson who first realised that the best sitcoms starred actors rather than comedians. My own experience showed that comedians tended to either exaggerate actions or insert their own jokes to get extra laughs. A prime example of this was a series first called *Tripper's Day* starring actor Leonard Rossiter as Norman Tripper, manager of a supermarket. Rossiter died during the making of the series and was replaced by comedian Bruce Forsyth as Cecil Slinger in the same role. It didn't work. Whereas Leonard Rossiter cleverly underplayed the part, Bruce Forsyth over played it, making his customary funny faces and asides which never really suited the character writer Brian Cooke created.

There are many familiar situations that have re-occurred in sitcom series. Here are a few you'll immediately recognise:

- The characters get trapped in a lift or accidentally locked in some confined space.

- One of the characters is writing his autobiography and the others are desperate to know what's being written about them.

- They are low on funds and argue about what each of them will have to sacrifice to save money.

- They book a bargain holiday which turns out to be a disaster.

- To keep fit they join a Health Club and all the strenuous exercise leaves them worse than they started.

- They arrange a surprise birthday party for one of the characters who surprises them by going off somewhere, because he thought nobody cared about him.

- An old friend comes for a short visit and overstays his welcome.

- To avoid a recent spate of burglaries they buy a huge dog which is hard to control and disrupts their lives.

- A character is in line for an inheritance which turns out to be much less than he had expected. And finally,

- a character who plays practical jokes on others has a practical joke played on him.

Those premises have been used countless times, but seem fresh when new characters are featured in them.

Let us take the latter situation and, instead of a practical joke, make it a scam. If we adopted the idea for *Fawlty Towers*, it could work out along these lines:

We'll start with Basil Fawlty lecturing his staff and some of the regular hotel guests to be aware of the many scams currently being perpetrated on ordinary people like themselves. Then he goes to the bank to collect the Fawlty Towers staff's wages and on his way back, falls for the old trick of separating two kids fighting in the street while one of them steals his wallet.

Realising he's been a victim of the kind of simple confidence trick he'd warned the others about, he now has to return to the hotel and face the wrath of his wife, Sybil. Basil is ashamed, but has an idea. He dishevels his clothes and tells Sybil he was mugged. "But you're six foot four, Basil." She says. "Surely you could have fought off a mugger."

"Yes," he agrees, "but there were six of them. Big wrestling types. A whole gang. I put up a fight, probably crippled a couple of them, but they finally overpowered me. There was nothing I could do."

"There is now" says Sybil. "We'll call the police!" And she does.

Now Basil, who had lied to Sybil, must compound it by lying to the police too. He is forced to give a fictitious description of what happened and help with identikit pictures of his supposed assailants. Next day he gets a call from the police to attend a police line-up to identify the suspected villains. Reluctantly he faces a dozen evil looking felons all glaring menacingly at him. He attempts to get out of it by feigning loss of memory due to the blow on the head he claims to have sustained during the mugging. But that doesn't get him off the hook, because the police say they'll call in a hypnotist to regress his memory back to the incident.

In an effort to thwart the hypnotist and avoid being put to sleep, Basil takes pep pills and several mugs-full off strong black coffee. The police say the hypnotist is now not available till the next day and Basil has yet again to take more pep pills and coffee, making himself a jittery, nervous wreck. He knows he faces the threat or being charged with perjury and wasting police time.

Meanwhile the hotel staff are on strike because they've not been paid and the guests are adding to Basil's problems by complaining about the poor service and threatening to pack their bags and leave.

This is all getting too much for Basil who decides he's had enough and will take the consequences of telling the police it was all a pack of lies. But before he can do so, the police come to him to say they know it was false because the hypnotist was conned by the same two kids who were arrested following his identikit description. In their premises they recovered Basil's missing wallet. Basil is let off with a stern warning never try to and fool the police again. I'd probably end with Basil happily telling Sybil that the panic is over, the police will forget it this time.

"Yes, Basil" she says threateningly, "But I won't!"

That plot typically shows how a little white lie can lead to more serious unforeseen problems for the liar.

A similar situation could have been concocted for Tony Hancock with his co-habiting partner Sid James. Probably that would start with Hancock stopping off at the Bookies to collect Sid's winnings after a successful bet.

Imagine Alf Garnett being investigated for suspected income benefit fraud, which he had not, in fact, committed. Protesting his innocence gets him nowhere and an Inspector is sent round to Alf's house to interrogate him. If that Inspector turns out to be a black man, ultra racist Alf would complain bitterly to his family and friends about "These bloody immigrants coming over here to accuse me, a loyal, law-abiding, through and through true British, hard working man, of fiddling!" He will, of course demand to speak to the Head Inspector who'll turn out to be Asian or Chinese.

Similarly so if a Black census taker turned up to ask about Alf's particulars including his Ethnic background. Anything that highlights the Garnett prejudices will be useful for an episode's plot line, but would always end with Alf having made a fool of himself though never backing down or apologising.

We could borrow one of the above-mentioned familiar storylines and have Alf Garnett receive a letter from a solicitor in Australia saying he is the only relative they can trace of a man who died over there without leaving a will. If he can prove who he is then he will be the sole beneficiary of the relative's estate. Alf goes to the Records office to trace any relationship he can find to the deceased and established that his great grandfather's criminal brother was deported to Australia and this recently-deceased man was his gay, unmarried grandson. The man is gay, of mixed race and is all the things Alf is prejudiced against. But there is money at stake and Alf is willing to set his prejudices aside in this instance. The man was a sheep farmer and Alf assumes he must have been very wealthy. "Probably too busy to find time to make a will."

So Alf will work out how he will spend the millions in his inheritance. He takes his mates out for a drink to celebrate, studies brochures of world cruises he intends to take and even looks at country mansions. In the end he will find that the criminal element of his great uncle had been passed down through the family and the lately deceased ran the farm as a cover for growing cannabis and all his assets had been confiscated by the Australian police. So instead of being rich, Alf is out of pocket for the treats he gave his friends and finally gets a sizeable bill from the solicitors who he denounces as being "Even worse crooks than my family."

In a *One Foot In The Grave* episode, Richard Wilson's character Victor Meldrew could be shopping in a supermarket when a shoplifter, realising he's being followed by a security guard, dumps his stolen whisky bottle into Victor's trolley without him knowing. The alarm goes off as Victor exits the supermarket and he is arrested for stealing the whisky. He was unaware that the real shoplifter had dumped the bottle in his trolley and cannot prove that he never drinks whisky and is meticulously honest.

He would be questioned by the shop's manager who is determined to make an example of Victor to deter other would-be shoplifters. To make this plot stronger we should start with Victor applying for membership of the local golf club or Rotarians so that any blemish on his character would disqualify him. Eventually, when he convinces the manager that he is innocent, he leaves the store only to find his car has now overstayed its allotted meter time and he has got a parking ticket. Rather than go through all that palaver of proving it wasn't his fault, he decides to pay the fine.

A storyline for *Only Fools And Horses* might have Rodney and Uncle Albert bemoan the fact they can't afford a holiday this year. Rodney says they *can* have a holiday in Spain for free. Well, at least the accommodation will be free; all they have to do is pay their air fare to Malaga. He refers to a circular he's received in the post looking for people to buy time-shares. The firm's representative will meet them at the airport and all they have to do is agree to look at a few places and the rest of their time is free to do what they want.

Sounds too good to be true and, of course it is. To start with Delboy tries to get them upgraded on the plane, but is unsuccessful. He tries flirting with the air stewardess, boasting about being in the property business and doing one of his regular trips to Spain to buy a block of flats...or two.

When they get to Spain the very pretty Rep takes them to their hotel, which looks great. But they find their apartment is in the annexe overlooking the dustbins. The plumbing works, but only when it wants to. They try to change rooms claiming it's bad for Uncle Albert's asthma, which he exaggerates. The hotel calls a doctor. Delboy thinks they are covered by their E111 card, but finds out they have shot themselves in the foot by claiming Albert's had his asthma prior to the holiday and had neglected to mention it on his insurance form. So they're already out of pocket.

They are in Fuengirola and plan to spend the next day sunbathing on the beach and eyeing the Bikini-clad girls as they go by. But that is not to be. The Rep has planned a full day of visiting half built flats which she tries to talk them into buying. Delboy has to keep thinking up reasons to turn each one down, including such things as they're north-facing and his Feng Shui says he must live facing South.

He finally hits on a plan agreeing to buy the next one and will pay for the deposit with a dud cheque. By the time they realise it, the Trotters will be out of the country and safely home. But they hadn't reckoned on their plane being delayed and the Rep's company's strong arm men come to the airport. Del and Co. hurriedly get on the next plane back to England, but hadn't noticed it's to Newcastle. When they arrive at Newcastle airport at four in the morning, minus their luggage, they are stuck there for 24 hours before they can get a plane back to Heathrow where they have parked the car. So their holiday was both disappointing and costly. At home Del opens a letter with a similar, hard to believe offer, which he immediately tears up.

On The Buses featured Reg Varney and Bob Grant as Bus Driver and Conductor respectively with Stephen Lewis as their arch enemy Blakey, the Bus Inspector who was determined never to let them pull the wool over his eyes. But in the end they always managed to outsmart him. In the background were Doris Hare as Reg's mother and always-squabbling Anna Karen and Michael Robbins as Reggie's live-in sister and brother-in-law Arthur and Olive.

My idea for a storyline for this series would have involved splitting up Bob and Reg by having Bob contract shingles or some such contagious disease and therefore confined to bed. As a temporary replacement, Reg is given a beautiful, sexy female bus conductor who is quite new to the job and happy to accept any advice or guidance Reg can offer her. He, of course, takes full advantage of this and meets her off duty in the evenings to teach her the tricks of the trade. She keeps flattering Reg who loves every minute of it.

He lies to Blakey that the new clippie is a great admirer of his and that she actually fancies him. Blakey is taken in by this and makes concessions to Reg and the girl that he would normally be dead against.

Reg visits the sick Bob several times and tries to convince him he needs more time off work to recover and recuperate after his illness. The real reason for this is that he wants to prolong his time working with the sexy clippie.

As a subplot, two things are happening. Firstly, Michael and Olga are arguing over money. Arthur is under threat of being made redundant and he wants Olive to get a job to help out with their finances. Secondly he borrows money off his mother-in-law to buy the latest state-of-the art camcorder that he has had his heart set on.

Reg borrows the camcorder to film Blakey in a compromising (though quite innocent) pose with the clippie. He is obviously intending a bit of blackmail to negotiate either a better route or a newer bus or better hours.

It could end with the girl placing the camera in a hidden position to take pictures of her and Reg together to show them to her wrestler-type boyfriend, thus blackmailing Reg into making up the shortages when she has spent some of the fares on luxuries for herself.

Reg has to backtrack on convincing Bob that he is really ill and tell him how remarkably well he now looks, just to get him back to work. Two things then happen to complete the story. One is that the clippie's boyfriend is secretly fed the picture of Blakey with the clippie which results in Blakey getting his eye blacked… and two, Olga gets a job as a replacement clippie and Reg, determined not to get lumbered with her, makes Bob promise never to get ill again.

For *Dad's Army* the story I would have offered might have had Mainwaring and his men being given a lecture on army manoeuvres by a Captain who used a set of model tin soldiers with tiny model cannons and tanks. He gives Mainwaring a text book of strategic battles and instructs him to study the book and, using tin models, to demonstrate them to the men.

Mainwaring is proud to have been chosen for this task and tells his men that they will soon be ready, if called upon, to outwit the enemy on all fronts. But, as he tells them, careless talk costs lives, so they will be sworn to secrecy.

Having read the first part of the book he uses the model set to show them a manoeuvre which, as Private Walker points out, has gaping big flaws in it. "You must have turned two pages over at once."

A local journalist overhears Privates Pike and Frazer talking about their lesson in engaging the enemy and senses he has the makings of a good story. He tries to follow it up with a phone call to Mainwaring which is answered by Corporal Jones who is left manning the office. The journalist poses as an official from the War Office and says he understands they have been given some new equipment and asks how it's working out. "Well" says Jones "the four armoured tanks are very good. The six 60 millimetre cannon are beautifully made. We're learning what to do with them tomorrow." "And you're not frightened by the prospect of using them?" enquires the writer. "Oh no, sir. As a matter of fact, we're all very excited. I mean, we've all just done our drilling and marching, but now we're going to get a crack at strategic manoeuvres. At last I feel like a real soldier."

"You say you have four armoured tanks and six 60 millimetre cannons. How many men do you have?"

"According to this sheet, sir. We have two platoons, that's roughly about one hundred men. Anything else you want to know, sir?"

" No thanks," says the journalist. "I think you've told me enough to be getting on with."

The next day the local paper's headline says Warmington-on-Sea is obviously the War Office's chosen point to launch the invasion of France. They are lining up lots of well trained soldiers and heavy artillery. One of the brave men I spoke to says they are eagerly looking forward to it."

Mainwaring reads this and thinks the information must have come from the War Office and therefore be true.

"They are lining us up for the great launch. Are we ready for it, men?" None of them is very keen. Walker says he would be happy to go, but his foot is playing up after he'd tripped over a Yank in the black-out. The only one claiming to be ready to fight the foe is Private Pike who says "It'll be an honour to die for my country. It's something I'll be able to tell my grandchildren about."

"Shut up, Pike. Stupid boy!"

A minister from the War Office comes down to find out where this story came from. Via the journalist he traces the source of the misunderstanding. Mainwaring apologises and is told that it could well come to be true. In case of a planned full scale invasion of France we WOULD rely on the Warmington-on-Sea Home Guard...... But only as a last resort.

So where do the ideas for storylines come from? As I have previously said, the best ones come from your own experiences. Perhaps an embarrassing incident or a moment when you triumphed over adversity or when something you'd been looking forward to turned out to be a disappointment. The little white lie that grew. When someone from your distant past turned up unexpectedly. When you took sides in an argument and made enemies of both participants.

I don't really want to put words into your own mouth. You know what your experiences have been and spending an hour or two listing the interesting ones you can remember could be time well spent. Once you have selected the experience you then set about the exaggerating process or imagining what might have happened if the end result had been different.

I have known writers pore through old copies of *The London Evening News* at the British Museum Library because in the 1950's and 1960's they had a short story every day. Some of these were the basic ideas for good sitcom episodes. I am not condoning stealing some other writer's ideas. But a good professional writer ought to be able to bend, stretch or rearrange an idea to create an original one of his own. Good ideas should inspire other good ideas.

No one criticises Leonard Bernstein and Stephen Sondheim for basing their musical *West Side Story* on Shakespeare's Romeo &

Juliet, or any of Rodgers & Hammerstein's musicals which were based on someone else's books. What they wrote was their own version of those stories.

The *Reggie Perrin* sitcom series was first written as a book by David Nobbs who then adapted it as a hit TV series. That is another route you may want to take, adapting a book, either your own or by another author who is either willing to co-operate with you in the writing or agrees to sell the TV rights.

But personally I think that if you can't find interesting stories based on your own life, you must have had a pretty dull life and should get out more. So your exercise for this lesson is to list three events in your life that you think can be developed into sitcom storylines. Then work at least one of them into a full storyline.

LESSON SEVEN. Sitcom Dialogue

Most of us are influenced by our background. A Cockney, for instance, will include rhyming slang in his speech. If he's hard of hearing he'll say, "I'm a bit mutt and Jeff", deaf. If he were off for a walk in the park, he'd say, "I'm going for a ball of chalk in the song and lark." Upstairs would be referred to as "Up the apples and pears." "'Eck as like", "Ee by gum." and saying moomy and poopy instead of mummy and puppy identifies a Yorkshire man. The Welsh, Irish and Scots also have their own vernacular expressions which add colour to their speech and reveal their origins.

An ex-naval man would include nautical terms in his speech. Likewise an ex-convict would use words like "lag", "porridge" and "snout." A youth would use modern slang terms like "Doing me 'ead in", "Real cool" and "Garage or Acid House parties." Peter Sellers, as the militant shop steward in *I'm Alright, Jack*, spoke in the terms of that office. A policeman giving evidence in court would speak in similar terms. These are all great assets in getting your viewers to know more about your characters. But do use them sparingly. Don't flood their speeches with these terms all the time as that would be going over the top and be too repetitious.

Unless you are writing the *Mr. Bean* type silent comedy sitcom, you need speeches for your characters. Speeches that tell us about the person delivering them and the situation they are in. And at the same time lead to laughs. Probably the most difficult task for the writer is the opening scene, especially of the initial episode when the audience are meeting your character(s) for the first time.

It is also essential that the TV company to whom you submit your script is gripped by the first few pages. That does not mean they have to be hilariously funny. In fact, it could be a hazard if you start too funny and can't sustain it. A rule I was taught early in my career is, if you can't be funny, at least be interesting. That first scene has to hold the audience's attention and leave them intrigued to know what happens next. The funniest film I ever saw was *Some Like It Hot* which got huge laughs, but only because the opening scene in which Jack Lemmon and Tony Curtis witness the St. Valentine's Day massacre. As long as that scene was taken seriously then the threat of being bumped off by the killers was real enough to make the consequential desperate acts of Lemmon and Curtis, funny. If that massacre scene had been funny the film would not have worked.

I recall seeing a one-off sitcom on American TV which may well have been inspired by that film. It began when a middle-aged man arrived in a taxi outside a suburban house. He paid the driver and carried his suitcases into the house. To his surprise a middle aged woman and a teenage boy and girl greeted him with "Hello Darling" and "Hi, Dad." The man was startled and asked "Who the hell are you? And what are you doing in my house?"

"We live here," said the woman. "I'm your wife and these are your teenage children."

"That's right," said the lad, "like you, we're all part of the witness protection scheme. I suppose we'd better introduce ourselves." In those few sentences we'd learnt that this sitcom was about a dysfunctional family. Four strangers forced to live together and put up with each other's foibles for fear of being hounded by criminals out for revenge.

The woman was overweight, the boy wore earrings and had tattoos and the girl was dressed in a mini skirt. As our man was obviously a smart-suited city type, the viewers instinctively knew they were not going to get along. To each member of this manufactured family the others were like aliens from another planet. Their enforced close proximity was bound to cause friction, yet they could not leave as they were in what's known in the profession as a "locked-in" situation.

Their friction, in the hands of a good comedy writer, easily provided laughs. That show had the perfect quick set-up for a sitcom.

Steptoe & Son, *Porridge* and *Open All Hours* all had the two main characters sharing the same abode. Harold and Albert Steptoe lived together because they were father and son. Arkwright and Granville shared accommodation behind the shop they ran together. Fletcher and Godber were literally locked in because they had to share a prison cell. Usually when a writer puts two such character together, he'd make one a schemer and the other his not-too-smart sidekick, confidant or accomplice. The latter's purpose is to act dumb and be told the opinions and proposed actions of the former. That way, the audience is indirectly being informed. The sidekick virtually represents the audience and will ask the questions they want answered.

In the 1960's I wrote a BBC Radio sitcom series called *Dishonest To Goodness* starring Bernard Bresslaw and John Bluthal as two brothers who try to pull off scams that always fail at the end. About fifteen years later John Sullivan created the TV series *Only Fools And Horses* on very similar lines. His Delboy Trotter (David Jason) was the schemer and dreamer and sibling Rodney (Nicholas Lyndhurst) was the dimwitted, manipulated accomplice.

The similarity can be gauged in this short opening scene from one of the radio episodes. As you read it you can probably imagine David Jason as John and Nicholas Lyndhurst as Bernie:

ANNOUNCER:

Welcome to *Dishonest To Goodness*, where we once again meet up with two of nature's finest fiddlers with only one thing in mind....making money.

BERNIE:

(A LONG INCOHERENT STREAM OF BABY TALK AND GURGLING)

JOHN:

(CONCERNED) Bernie, are you alright?

BERNIE:

I'm just practicing. You know where I'm going?

JOHN:

To the mad house, by the sound of it.

BERNIE:

No. I'm going round to the Johnson's. I'm babysitting for them tonight.

JOHN:

(LAUGHS) YOU'RE babysitting. What do YOU know about babies?

BERNIE:

A lot. After all, I used to be one. Anyway I read a book all about babies.

JOHN:

Oh yeah? What's it called?

BERNIE:

"What Every Expectant Mother Should Know." It's got a diet sheet at the back, so I got all the food to take with me. Milk stout…calcium pills….pickles….

JOHN:

You nit, that's for the mother! The baby just has milk.

BERNIE:

I'll get some on the way. I'm taking a book along to read to the baby too. Look, it's Goldilocks And The Three Bears.

JOHN: Their baby is only six months old. She won't want to hear that.

BERNIE:

I'll take it anyway.

JOHN:

Why?

BERNIE:

I want to hear it.

JOHN:

I think I'd better come along too.

BERNIE:

What for?

JOHN:

To watch BOTH babies! How much are they paying you for this?

BERNIE:

Five quid an hour. It'll be the easiest money I ever earned.

JOHN:

Correction – WE ever earned. I'm coming too.

Those few speeches set up the characters and the storyline for that particular episode in which John and Bernie build up a mass babysitting agency which collapses with an outbreak of infectious measles which spreads not just to the tiny tots, but to the brothers themselves.

Dialogue can convey an attitude. If, for instance, one character calls another by their first name we know they are on familiar friendly terms. "Listen Fred, I want to tell you something…" But if they use the full name it depicts anger "Listen Fred Timpson, I want to tell you something…." If a character thinks another has been too generous or extravagant he wouldn't use the person's real name at all. He's say something like "Listen Mr. Rockefeller, don't be so free with our money…"

Playwright Neil Simon never invented sarcasm, but he has made more money from it than any one I know. If you examine his dialogue you'll find that he creates situations where his characters are angry and are sarcastic to each other. It was those sarcastic lines that got the loudest laughs. It was comedian/writer Mel Brooks that said, "Anger fuels comedy."

Neil Simon shows controlled anger, leading to sarcasm, in the opening scene of *Come Blow Your Horn* where he quickly establishes the strained relationship between a businessman and his errant, playboy son who's been away skiing when he should have been courting a particular client:

FATHER:

For two days he's been sitting waiting in the Hotel Croydon while you're playing in the snow.

ALAN:

Dad, I promise you, I won't lose the account.

FATHER:

Why? This would be the first one you ever lost? You want to see the list? You could ski (GESTURES) down your cancellations.

ALAN:

I couldn't get back in time, Dad. Skiing had nothing to do with it.

FATHER:

I'm sorry, I forgot. I left out golf and sailing   and sleeping and drinking and women. You are terrific. If I was in the bum business I would want ten like you.

ALAN:

That's not true. I put in plenty of time in the business.

FATHER:

Two years. In six years you put in two years. I had my bookkeeper figure it out.

ALAN:

Thank you.

FATHER:

My own son. I get more help from my competitors.

In those few short speeches we have learned that Alan is a ne'er-do-well playboy who will have to change his lifestyle or lose his job.

In the TV series *Porridge* almost all of Fletcher's lines had a tinge of sarcasm. Many were aimed directly at the victim, others delivered as asides. Ronnie Barker's Arkwright in *Open All Hours* also spoke sarcastically to his customers as well as his nephew, Granville. To avoid making the characters too similar, Barker gave Arkwright a stutter and Northern accent.

Delboy in *Only Fools And Horses* tried to put on an air of sophistication, but all-too-often shot himself in the foot by using a mispronunciation or a similar-but-wrong word to get a laugh. He'd say something like, "There's too much crime about. If they brought back capital punishment that would be a detergent." or "What I'm selling you here is the genuine article. It's worth more than the Pope diamond." or "I went to see that Shakespeare play *Two Gentlemen Of Veruka*." It's a useful device when you need a break from serious dialogue in a plot-setting scene. It has to, of course, be in keeping with the character that says it.

In the series *Here's Harry*, written by Vince Powell and Frank Roscoe, comedy actor Harry Worth played a painfully innocent, gormless character utterly confused by life's every-day events. Vince Powell suggested I quote the following scene to illustrate Harry's muddled thinking...

FADE UP ON INTERIOR OF SMALL POST OFFICE. DAY.

IT IS THE TYPE OF POST OFFICE ONE MIGHT SEE ANYWHERE – A LONG COUNTER WITH ITS SEPARATION OF WIRE MESH STANDING AT RIGHT ANGLES TO THE DOOR. OPPOSITE THE COUNTER IS A POLISHED TABLE

WITH ITS USUAL COLLECTION OF INKWELL AND G.P.O. PENS. THE CLERK - A SLIM NONDESCRIPT TYPE OF FELLOW - IS JUST SERVING A STOCKY NEWSPAPER SELLER, BILL.

CLERK:

(HANDING OVER A POSTAL ORDER) There you are, Sir. Two-and- sixpenny postal order and a threepenny stamp – that'll be three shillings altogether.

BILL:

(PAYING) Three bob – here you are.

CLERK: Thank you, sir.

BILL MOVES OFF TO SIT AT THE TABLE. HARRY ENTERS AND MOVES TO THE COUNTER.

HARRY:

(CHEERFULLY) Ah, good morning. I wonder if you could help me?

CLERK:

(PLEASANTLY) Postal order or stamps?

HARRY:

A pin.

CLERK:

(TAKEN ABACK) A pin?

HARRY:

Yes. Preferably a safety pin, one with a blunt point. It's for my (WAVING HIS COUPON) football pools.

CLERK:

Oh. You want a pin for your football pools?

HARRY:

Yes. I used to select my teams by using the ages of my friends. For example, Mr. Jones the postman is thirty three and on the coupon that's Watford. Mrs. Williams is fifty one and that's Kilmarnock.

CLERK:

So you're moving over to the pin method now.

HARRY:

Unfortunately I've had to change my system since Auntie's birthday this year. You see there are only sixty teams on the coupon.

CLERK:

(NODDING) Oh, I see what you mean, your Auntie is now sixty one.

HARRY:

No. Sixty five.

CLERK:

(INCREDULOUS) Sixty five!

HARRY:

Yes. (LOOKING ROUND, THEN LEANING OVER TO WHISPER) She lies about her age. (THE CLERK REACTS) How old are you?

CLERK;

(SARCASTICALLY) I was thirty five, but I'm feeling a bit older, now.

HARRY:

(UNAWARE OF THE SARCASM, LOOKING AT HIS COUPON) Thirty five? Rochdale. What a pity. That was the milkman.

If you are old enough to remember Harry Worth on TV (when a postage stamp was just threepence), you'll picture the comedy actor actually saying those lines.

No one is going to believe that those characters were based on real people. It was a hit nevertheless, in common with other sitcom series in which the characters were unbelievable, but funny all the same. They include *Father Ted* featuring a drunken priest, *The Peter Principal* with an incompetent Bank Manager, *My Hero* and *Mork & Mindy* as aliens from outer space, *So Haunt Me* starring a ghost, *Mr. Ed*, a talking horse and Maxwell Smart as an accident prone secret agent in *Get Smart*.

The writers of those series managed to sell those scripts to television companies, proving that the golden rule of "truth in comedy" can sometimes be successfully broken. However you are more likely to get your script accepted if the audience can identify with your main character(s).

When scriptwriter Johnny Speight lectured to my students he was asked for an example of uncontrolled anger. He chose the following dialogue he'd written that very day for an episode of Till Death Us Do Part in which the Garnett family are on a train heading for Bournemouth for their annual holiday...

ALF:

Bloody go-slow! Ain't it marvellous, eh? This bloody train ain't hardly moved for half an hour.

RITA:

Oh shut up, Dad.

ALF:

Well, makes yer sick, dunnit? The only sunny day we've had this year and we've got to spend it sitting in a bloody railway carriage. (SEES TICKET COLLECTOR IN CORRIDOR) Hoi! When's this bloody train gonna get a move on?

COLLECTOR:

I dunno..

ALF:

We left Waterloo an hour ago and we ain't even passed Clapham yet. (POINTS TO WINDOW) You could still see Waterloo out of here. I could walk faster.

COLLECTOR:

Well, why don't yer?

ALF:

Look, I don't want no bloody cheek out of you. I paid my bloody fare, I have, mate and I expect a bit of servility. I mean, it's alright having go-slows when you're going to work. I mean half of them don't mind that. Lazy sods. But we're going on a bloody holiday, mate. I mean, we're sitting here in our own time, we are, not the bloody guvnor's. No bloody lunch, we ain't had. Probably miss our tea as well.

COLLECTOR:

They're serving tea in the buffet car.

ALF:

Yer, so they might be. But if we have tea here we've got to pay for it, ain't we?

COLLECTOR:

Yer, of course you have. You don't expect us to give you tea for nothing, do you?

ALF:

But our tea's already paid for in Bournemouth, in our hotel where we're staying.

MIKE:

Look here. (PUTS HIS HAND IN HIS POCKET) Go and buy a cup of tea. I mean, blimey!

ALF:

I don't wanna buy a cup of tea on here. If you bought one you wouldn't be able to drink it. They see you with a cup of tea in your hand and they start going fast, and jumping and jerking, so you spill it all over. I know 'em, bloody idle Labour rubbish!

As Johnny Speight explained, he'd made Alf Garnett not only a loudmouth, but also totally arrogant and insensitive to other people's feelings. In essence he was as nasty a character as Basil Fawlty in *Fawlty Towers*, but both men were acceptable because of their vulnerability that came from their being continually belittled by their wives.

An American TV Company bought the format of *Till Death Us Do Part* and produced their own version called *All In The Family* with Brooklyn's Archie Bunker as the intolerant racist who told an Afro-American "Look, I ain't no bigot! I'm the first to say – it ain't your fault you're coloured."

To highlight the racist angle, producer Norman Lear gave Archie a black family as neighbours. When required by the storyline, Lionel the Black neighbour, got laughs by taunting Archie about the bigotry he always swiftly denied…

ARCHIE:

Lionel, we're friends, ain't we?

LIONEL:

And neighbours! We live right next to each other.

ARCHIE:

Yeah. Yeah. I know all about that. But gettin' back to bein' friends, I need your help.

LIONEL:

You got something heavy for me to carry, Mr. Bunker?

Like Hancock, Archie Bunker always felt the whole world was against him. In one scene he was wrongly convinced the FBI. were spying on him and suspected everyone that came near his house…

EDITH:

(LOOKING OUT THE WINDOW) I don't see nobody.

ARCHIE:

Of course not, Edith! Them FBI guys is experts at keeping hidden.

EDITH:

Then how do you know they're watching?

ARCHIE:

If they wasn't watching, you could see 'em. If you can't see 'em, then they're watchin'. See?

EDITH:

Oh!

ARCHIE:

Hey, look at that there. I ain't never seen that car on this block! That could be them! Huh, Edith!

EDITH:

You mean – the one with the lady and the three children getting out?

GLORIA:

(SARCASTICALLY) That could be them, Daddy. I hear they're masters of disguise.

ARCHIE:

Well, they are – they're tricky.

Perhaps the best known angry character on American TV was Jackie Gleason as Ralph Kramden, the obese New York bus driver who was always trying to better himself. Unlike our own Hattie Jacques or Les Dawson who never mentioned their excess girth, this series deliberately made a feature of it. Alice, Ralph's wife, used it as a weapon whenever she wanted to get back at him.

ALICE:

(EXASPERATED) Ralph, you're nothing but a… but a… but a grouchy old crab!

RALPH:

I'm a what?

ALICE:

A grouchy old crab.

RALPH:

(SMUGLY) Sticks and stones may break my bones, but names'll never hurt me.

ALICE:

Neither will sticks and stones. They couldn't get through the blubber!

As the old saying goes, ignorance is bliss. It also provides some great laughs. But it's essential the audience believes the character really is ignorant. No dumb blonde was ever more convincing that Gracie Allen in the *Burns and Allen* TV series. Her main gimmick was illogical logic.

GEORGE:

What's that?

GRACIE:

Electric cords. I had them shortened. This one's for the iron, this one's for the floor lamp.

GEORGE:

Why did you shorten them?

GRACIE:

To save electricity.

Gracie also scored well misinterpreting what others said:

GRACIE:

The night before last, George came home from the office feeling terrible.

BLANCHE:

Probably flu.

GRACIE:

No, he drove the car.

The opposite was the case with Ronnie Barker's Norman Stanley Fletcher in *Porridge*. Fletcher ruled the roost in the cell he shared with young lag, Godber. In addition to being a dyed-in-the-wool cynic, he was very manipulative. A trait Phil Silvers had in abundance as *Sgt. Bilko*. Fletcher was able to get strict disciplinarian prison warder Mr. MacKay to inadvertently bend to his wishes. Whereas Bilko's and even Delboy's shenanigans wound up in failure, Fletcher's were mostly successful. He always had the last word or defiant gesture. It's interesting to note that the spin off series called *Going Straight* in which Fletcher returned to civilian life, only survived one short series, proving the character only worked when in a locked-in situation.

In *Steptoe & Son* the two rag-and-bone merchants were always at loggerheads, but stood together when need be to fight any outsider that invaded their domain. They were father and son, but completely different in appearance and temperament. Albert was shabbily dressed, dirty and canny to the point of being ruthless. Harold, on the other hand, was an innocent with frustrated ambitions to better himself. Though, at times the old man disgusted him, Harold could not bring himself to desert his Dad and Galton & Simpson's scripts reflected their hidden family bond.

A popular shortcut for sitcom writers is to begin with a telephone conversation. In this example Lois, who is madly in love with her Boss, would start each episode on the phone to her telephone operator friend Rita, setting up the situation. At the point where she'd outlined the beginning of the story for that week, her Boss would arrive and the phone conversation would come to an abrupt end. This script example quickly defines the relationship between Lois and Richard Bradley, her Boss.

CLOSE-UP OF DOOR WITH SIGN SAYING "RICHARD BRADLEY – PRIVATE INVESTIGATOR".

MIX THROUGH TO:

INTERIOR LOIS'S OFFICE. MORNING.

AS THE SHOW OPENS. LOIS IS SPEAKING ON THE TELEPHONE TO HER FRIEND RITA. SHE HAS THE PHONE RESTING BETWEEN HER SHOULDER AND EAR AND IS OPENING THE MORNING MAIL AT THE SAME TIME.

LOIS:

No, Rita…it's alright, I can talk to you. I'm not too busy at the moment. So how did your date go last night?......He was a thorough gentleman? I know what you mean. I had a lousy evening as well. Didn't he even kiss you goodnight?

FROM HEREON CAMERA INTERCUTS BETWEEN RITA AND LOIS AT THE DIRECTOR'S DISCRETION. RITA IS SEATED AT AN OFFICE SWITCHBOARD AND IS OBVIOUSLY A TELEPHONE OPERATOR.

RITA:

No. I gave him a hint. I stood there for quarter of an hour in the cold with my lips puckered.

LOIS:

And he didn't notice?

RITA:

He noticed alright. He asked if I had any Zulu blood in my family.

LOIS:

(LAUGHS) I shouldn't laugh. After all I'm in the same boat…and it's sinking fast.

RITA:

Richard?

LOIS:

Yes. (LOOKS AT PICTURE OF HIM ON WALL) I'm still mad about him and he hasn't even noticed I'm a woman.

RITA:

Have you tried changing your make-up?

LOIS:

Yes. On Monday I came to the office wearing the same make-up as Twiggy.

RITA:

That didn't spur him into action?

LOIS:

Yes, he gave me the day off. He said I looked ill.

Having set up the relationship, the Boss's first words would plant the show's storyline. "Get off that phone, Lois, we've work to do. A client's just phoned wanting us to tail his wife. She's been frequenting a sleazy nightclub and he thinks she's having an affair with the owner. You may have to pose as a stripper."

Sexual role reversal can be a tool for comedy if you consider the Jennifer Saunders scripts for Absolutely Fabulous to be the female version of Simon Nye's *Men Behaving Badly*. It's the shock value that makes it funny. Let me demonstrate the point with a few lines of dialogue where the man assumes the natural role as seducer. In this scene Ed, the husband, sneaks up on his wife Shirley in the kitchen as she is about to serve their evening meal. He kisses her affectionately on the back of her neck.

SHIRLEY:

Careful! This pot is hot.

ED:

So am I. It isn't every day I get to celebrate a tenth wedding anniversary. Come here.

HE TURNS HER ROUND TO FACE HIM AND KISSES HER ON THE LIPS. THE KISS STARTS TO GET PASSIONATE AS SHE PUSHES HIM AWAY WITH HER KITCHEN-GLOVED HANDS.

SHIRLEY:

(GOOD NATUREDLY) Ed, there's a time and place for everything.

ED:

(LOOKS AT HIS WATCH) Agreed. The time is now seven thirty. You name the place.

SHIRLEY:

(SIGHS) I don't know what I'm going to do with you.

ED:

I've some good ideas.

SHIRLEY:

You're incorrigible.

ED:

So incorrige me!

That would be the start of a normal, romantic domestic scene. But let us imagine what the dialogue might be if we were to write a sitcom where the female was the sexual predator. If cast right, it should provide laughs.

Here is the first scene of a sitcom that gives a good example of role reversal where the female is the sexual predator.

ELLEN & EDDIE'S BEDROOM. NIGHT.

ELLEN AND EDDIE ARE IN BED. SHE IS RESTLESS AND AWAKE. HE IS ASLEEP AND SNORING LOUDLY. ELLEN SHAKES EDDIE. HE WAKES UP IN A PANIC.

EDDIE:

(ALARMED) What's wrong? Is it a burglar?   Is there a noise in the sitting room?

ELLEN:

No, the noise is in here. You're snoring!

EDDIE:

Oh, sorry. It's because I'm lying on my back. I'll turn over.

HE TURNS AWAY FROM HER TO LIE ON HIS SIDE.

ELLEN:

Don't turn away. I want to talk.

EDDIE:

(LOOKS AT BEDSIDE CLOCK) At two in the morning? Alright, you talk. But keep it quiet, because I'll be sleeping.

EDDIE SETTLES DOWN TO SLEEP AGAIN. ELLEN TURNS THE LIGHT ON.

ELLEN:

Eddie, when did we last make love?

EDDIE:

(STARTLED BY THE QUESTION) What?

ELLEN:

When did you last hold me in your arms?

EDDIE:

(CAN'T BELIEVE WHAT HE IS HEARING) When did I what?

ELLEN:

When did you last fondly caress me?

EDDIE:

You've been reading those Mills & Boon books again, haven't you? Look, will you please turn that light off! I feel like I'm getting the third degree here.

ELLEN:

Eddie Frazer, I am not turning the light OFF, until I've turned you ON!

SHE PUTS A HAND ON HIS SHOULDER. HE PUSHES IT OFF.

EDDIE:

Look, I'm very tired. I've had a hard day at the office, and if I don't get some sleep, it'll be even harder tomorrow.

ELLEN:

I'll settle for a kiss. Make me feel like a blushing bride again. Like on our wedding night.

EDDIE:

Oh, alright.

HE LEANS ACROSS AND GIVES HER A PECK ON THE CHEEK.

ELLEN:

(DISAPPOINTED) That's like our wedding night? Then what on earth did I have to blush about? (WORRIED) Eddie, is there something wrong with me?

EDDIE:

(TRYING TO SLEEP) Yes. There is.

ELLEN:

What?

EDDIE:

You talk too much.

ELLEN:

Eddie, we obviously have a communication problem and I want it solved. Right now!

EDDIE:

Well phone an Agony Aunt. Wake HER up at two in the morning! Now, Goodnight!

BUT SHE WON'T LET HIM SLEEP.

ELLEN:

You've changed since we got married. You no longer buy me flowers. You don't buy me chocolates……

EDDIE:

How about if I buy you some sleeping pills?! Ellen, I need my rest.

ELLEN:

I want to finish this discussion.

EDDIE:

Well go to sleep and take it up with me in your dreams.

EDDIE ALMOST MANAGES TO FALL ASLEEP.

ELLEN:

(AN ULTIMATUM) Eddie Fraser, either I get some hot passion or you get a cold breakfast!

SHE WAITS FOR A REPLY, BUT EDDIE IS NOW FAST ASLEEP AND SNORING.

FADE OUT..

Another prime example of where the sexual role reversal got big laughs was in *George & Mildred*, the TV series Johnnie Mortimer and Brian Cooke wrote for Brian Murphy and Yootha Joyce as a middle aged couple frustratingly fighting the battle of the sexes with invective as their chief weapon.

Originally they were just two characters in *Man About The House*, but were so strong they spun off into a series of their own with the format sold to American TV as The Ropers. Here are some choice insults that peppered the George & Mildred episode entitled *Baby Talk*.

When the young child Tristram asks George, "Will you read me a story?"

The somewhat reluctant George answers, "I dunno."

Tristram holds up a book and, referring to its title, says, "What about The Wicked Witch?"

George, getting his dig in about Mildred, answers, "Yeah, you get her to read you one."

Later, when Mildred returns to the Living Room after putting the child to bed she finds George asleep in front of the telly. She shakes him awake and says about Tristram, "He's asleep."

"So was I" says George.

"He kissed me goodnight."

To which George replies "He probably didn't have his glasses on."

134

Mildred confides in a friend she'd like a baby and considers adopting one. "It seems the only way." she says. "I don't think George is going to strike oil after all these years. The bit on the drill has grown blunt by now."

George is against the idea and when Mildred suggests IVF treatment he says, "You're talking about artificial insinuation."

When George takes his trousers off in front of a female guest, she says, "Don't worry about me, I'm not easily shocked."

To which Mildred replies "It's not shock I'm afraid of, love, it's pity ."

At the Adoption Society Mildred is asked her age. She says "Thirty five….and a few months."

"How many months?"

Under his breath George says "About a hundred."

When asked what other information the man at the Adoption Society probed about, Mildred says, "He just asked me questions about this, that and the other. I answered about this and that, but with George I was too embarrassed to confess about the other."

Your exercise for this lesson is to create a situation that would cause conflict between Basil and Sybil Fawlty, Harold and Albert Steptoe or George and Mildred Roper. Then write a scene showing how their argument begins.

LESSON EIGHT – A Sitcom Script.

After writing many sketch shows for top Dutch comedian Andre Van Duin (including the Netherlands' entry for the Golden Rose Festival), I was commissioned to provide the script for a sitcom with Andre as the star. My only brief was that his favourite British TV series were *Some Mothers Do 'Ave 'Em* in which Michael Crawford performed a lot of visual comedy and *The Good Life* which had the clash between the lower and upper class neighbours. I was instructed to attempt to combine the best elements of those two series. So I made the connection between the two married couples the fact that the wives were sisters. It was called *Being Neighbourly*.

Here's the first draft of the first episode script entitled *Unhandy Andy*. (I later sold this script in Canada, too.)

BEING NEIGHBOURLY

EPISODE NO. 1

'UNHANDY ANDY'

1st DRAFT

EPISODE ONE

Characters:
Andy Brock
Claire Brock
Frank Leeson
Rita Leeson
Mr. Elton (The Decorator)

Sets:

Adjoining back gardens of both houses
The Leesons' Living Room
The Brocks' Living Room
The Leesons' bedroom

Written by:

Brad Ashton

A Michael Steele and
    Frank Peppiatt Production
207 Erskine Avenue
Toronto, Ontario
Canada, M4P 1Z5
416—482—2867
in association with
Brad Ashton
©Copyright

'UNHANDY ANDY'

EPISODE ONE: BEING NEIGHBOURLY

NOTE: THE ENTIRE ACTION IN THIS EPISODE TAKES PLACE IN THE HOUSES OF TWO COUPLES, ANDY AND CLAIRE BROCK AND THEIR NEXT DOOR NEIGHBOURS FRANK AND RITA LEESON. THE TWO HOUSES ARE IDENTICAL IN SHAPE AND SIZE. BUT THEY ARE QUITE DIFFERENT IN THE WAY THEY ARE FURNISHED AND DECORATED. THE LEESONS ARE THE WEALTHIER COUPLE AND THEIR HOUSE AND GARDEN IS MUCH BETTER FURNISHED AND TASTEFULLY DECORATED. THE GARDEN IS LANDSCAPED AND WELL KEPT.

AFTER THE OPENING CREDITS

FADE THROUGH TO:

THE BROCKS' BACK GARDEN. DAY.

IT IS NOT A WELL KEPT GARDEN AND HAS MORE WEEDS THAN ACTUAL FLOWERS. NEITHER ANDY BROCK NOR HIS WIFE CLAIRE ARE KEEN GARDENERS. AS WE COME UP ON THEM, WE FIND THAT ANDY IS SURROUNDED BY PIECES OF WOOD OF VARIOUS SIZES THAT HAVE COME OUT OF A LARGE BOX. ON THE SIDE OF THE BOX IS A PICTURE OF A GARDEN SHED AND THE LABEL ON THE BOX SHOWS THAT IT IS A "DO-IT-YOURSELF" KIT FOR BUILDING A GARDEN SHED. ALSO ON THE GROUND ARE SEVERAL TOOLS, INCLUDING A POWERFUL ELECTRIC SAW. ANDY IS LOOKING AT THE WOOD AS HE IS JOINED BY CLAIRE.

CLAIRE:

Why must you be so stubborn, Andy? You've never built a garden shed before. We could have got a ready-made shed for only fifty dollars more.

ANDY:

I'm not like Frank next door, with plenty of money to throw around. In my vocabulary the words 'only' and 'fifty' don't belong in the same sentence. I've managed to borrow the tools and I'll build this shed myself.

CLAIRE:

No you won't. You'll just make a mess which I'll have the job of clearing up afterwards.

ANDY

Claire Brock, you're doing it again. Always putting me down when I attempt to do anything. I've read the instructions and a kid of five could build this shed.

CLAIRE:

Well you'd better bring him in to show you.

ANDY:

Just go back in the house and attend to your woman's work and leave a man to do what a man's got to do (HANDS HER THE WIRE LEAD OF THE ELECTRIC SAW) And plug this in as you go.

CLAIRE:

Alright, but I'm warning you Andy, if you cut your leg off with that saw, don't come running to me.

CLAIRE GOES INTO THE HOUSE.

ANDY:

(ANGRILY TO HIMSELF)   She never thinks I can do anything.

HE PICKS UP THE DETAILED INSTRUCTIONS THAT CONTAIN A DIAGRAM OF HOW TO BUILD THE SHED. HE TURNS THE INSTRUCTIONS UPSIDE DOWN AND THEN SEVERAL OTHER ANGLES. IT'S CLEAR HE DOESN'T UNDERSTAND IT AT ALL. HE SCRATCHES HIS HEAD.

PAN ACROSS TO:

THE LEESONS' GARDEN. DAY

THE TWO GARDENS ARE SEPARATED BY JUST A WOODEN FENCE. RITA LEESON IS STANDING NEXT TO THE FENCE AND DOWN AT A GROUP OF BEAUTIFUL LONG-STEMMED TULIPS GROWING THERE.

FRANK: (VOICE OVER)

Move in just a little closer, Rita. (SHE MOVES CLOSER TO THE TULIPS) That's just fine.

CAMERA PULLS OUT TO INCLUDE FRANK LEESON ,WHO IS STANDING NEXT TO A CAMERA MOUNTED ON A TRIPOD.

FRANK:

I'll just check to see it the light's O.K. Home & Gardens won't use the picture unless it's exactly right.

HE HOLDS UP HIS LIGHT METER AND IS SATISFIED THE READING IS O.K.

FRANK:

It's fine. I'll just get into position, but I don't want you to take it until I say I'm ready.

THEY EXCHANGE POSITIONS. RITA GETS BEHIND THE CAMERA AND FRANK GOES TO THE FENCE AND POSES, LOOKING DOWN LOVINGLY ON THE TULIPS.

FRANK:

Put your finger on the button. I'll count to three and then say 'ready'. One...Two...

BUT HE GETS NO FURTHER. WE HEAR THE SOUND OF A POWERFUL ELECTRIC SAW STARTING UP NEXT DOOR IN THE BROCKS' GARDEN AND A SPRAY OF SAWDUST COMES OVER THE GARDEN FENCE FALLING ALL OVER THE TULIPS. FRANK IS FURIOUS. HE TURNS TO LOOK OVER THE GARDEN FENCE AND GETS MORE SAWDUST OVER HIS HAIR AND SHOULDERS.

ANDY HAS HIS BACK TO FRANK AND IS SO BUSY SAWING A PLANK OF WOOD THAT HE DOES NOT HEAR FRANK YELLING AT HIM.

FRANK:

Turn that thing off!

CAMERA FOLLOWS FRANK AS HE GOES THROUGH THE
GATE THAT SEPARATES THE TWO GARDENS. HE
FOLLOWS THE WIRE LEAD AND PULLS IT OUT OF ITS
SOCKET. THE ELECTRIC SAW IMMEDIATELY STOPS
WORKING. ANDY HAS NOT SEEN THE PLUG BEING
PULLED OUT AND WONDERS WHY THE SAW HAS
SUDDENLY STOPPED. HE SHAKES IT AND TURNS THE
SWITCH ON AND OFF. BY NOW FRANK HAS REACHED
ANDY AND ANDY TURNS AND SEES HIM.

ANDY:

Ah, hello Frank. (RECRUITING HIS HELP) Do you know anything
about electric saws? This one's stopped working.

FRANK:

(REFERRING TO THE SAWDUST ON HIS HAIR AND
SHOULDERS) Look at me!

ANDY:

Tch. Tch. You must do something about that dandruff.

FRANK:

(SHOUTING) It's not dandruff, you idiot! I'm covered in your
sawdust. And look what you've done to my tulips.

FRANK DRAGS ANDY, BY THE SHOULDERS, OVER TO THE
FENCE.

FRANK:

You've ruined them.

ANDY LOOKS DOWN AT THE SAWDUST COVERED TULIPS.

ANDY:

Don't worry, I can soon fix that.

FRANK WATCHES AS ANDY GOES INTO HIS HOUSE AND COMES OUT WITH A SMALL BATTERY-OPERATED VACUUM CLEANER.

ANDY LEANS OVER THE FENCE AND SWITCHES ON THE VACUUM CLEANER JUST ABOVE THE TULIPS.

FRANK:

(ALARMED) What are you doing? Are you mad?!

ANDY TURNS OFF THE VACUUM CLEANER AND WE NOW SEE THAT IT HAS SUCKED THE TULIP FLOWERS OFF THE STEMS.

FRANK:

(NEAR TO TEARS) Oh, no!!

ANDY HANDS FRANK SOME OF THE TULIP FLOWERS THAT WERE STUCK TO THE VACUUM CLEANER.

ANDY:

Here, hold these. I'll go get some glue.

ANDY GOES BACK TO THE HOUSE. FRANK LOOKS AT THE REMAINS OF HIS PRIZE FLOWERS AND THROWS THEM ON THE GROUND IN A FURY.

FADE OUT

FADE UP ON:

THE LIVING ROOM OF THE BROCKS' HOUSE. DAY.

THE ADEQUATELY FURNISHED AND DECORATED LIVING ROOM SHOWS NO SENSE OF REAL TASTE. IT'S VERY WORKING CLASS, INCLUDING THE STANDARD PRINT PAINTINGS THAT ADORN THE PAINTED (NOT WALL PAPERED) WALLS. THERE ARE THREE DOORS LEADING OFF. ONE IS THE FRONT DOOR OF THE HOUSE. THE SECOND IS THE DOOR TO THE BATHROOM AND THE THIRD LEADS OFF TO THE KITCHEN. THERE IS A STAIRCASE THAT LEADS UPSTAIRS TO THE BEDROOM.

THE TWO WIVES, CLAIRE AND RITA, ARE HAVING
AFTERNOON TEA.

CLAIRE:

Another slice of cake, Rita?

RITA:

I shouldn't really, but it's so delicious.

CLAIRE:

And take a slice for your Frank, as a sort of peace offering for that
incident with Andy and the flowers yesterday.

RITA:

Oh, I'm sure Frank has forgotten that already. He's got more
important things on his mind. You know he recently got accepted as a
member of the Country Club?

CLAIRE:

Yes, he was very proud of that.

RITA:

Now he's even prouder. The Chairman himself phoned Frank
personally this morning. The Club's having some building work done
and they're asking some of the members to temporarily look after the
antiques they keep in their trophy room, and he's asked Frank to be
one.

CLAIRE:

(WITH A SMILE, OBVIOUSLY KIDDING) One of the antiques?

RITA:

(ALSO SMILING) No, silly, he's not that old. They're bringing round
whatever it is we're to look after this afternoon.

CLAIRE:

Will you have room, you've already got more antiques than anyone I
know? (WISTFULLY) I wish we had some but it's impossible with
Andy. He's so clumsy, nothing lasts long enough to get old.

RITA:

By the way, how did Andy get on with that shed? Did he finish it?

CLAIRE:

Sort of. Look for yourself. He's still trying to figure out how the door came to be on the roof.

CAMERA CUTS TO THEIR POINT OF VIEW THROUGH THE WINDOW.

ANDY HAS HIS HEAD AND SHOULDERS POPPING OUT THROUGH THE DOOR IN THE ROOF OF THE GARDEN SHED. IT IS BUILT VERY HAPHAZARDLY AND IS NOT THE RIGHT SHAPE AT ALL. ANDY IS SCRATCHING HIS HEAD.

WE HEAR CLAIRE AND RITA LAUGHING. WE CUT BACK TO THEM.

CLAIRE:

Next he wants to decorate this room. We need the walls painted. But I'm calling in a professional to do it.

RITA:

You're asking Andy to spend money? I bet he's angry about that.

CLAIRE:

He hasn't said a word about it. Mind you, there's a good reason. I haven't told him yet. I'm dreading it when Mr. Elton comes round this evening to quote us a price for the job.

CLAIRE SIPS HER TEA WITH A WORRIED LOOK ON HER FACE.

FADE OUT

FADE IN ON:

THE LIVING ROOM OF THE LEESONS' HOUSE. DAY.

THE ROOM IS VERY TASTEFULLY DECORATED WITH EXPENSIVE WALLPAPER, CURTAINS AND CARPETS. AROUND THE WALLS ARE REPRODUCTIONS OF FAMOUS PAINTINGS BY THE MASTERS. THERE IS A BOOKSHELF WITH ENCYCLOPAEDIAS AND BOOKS ON THE ARTS AND ALSO MANY ORNAMENTS MADE OF IVORY OR ONYX OR JADE. THE FURNITURE IS MOSTLY OLD FRENCH STYLE. ABOUT ONE YARD FROM THE FRONT DOOR IS A MARBLE PEDESTAL ON WHICH STANDS A LARGE CHINESE VASE.

THE CAMERA PULLS BACK FROM A CLOSE-UP OF THAT VASE AS WE OPEN THE SCENE.

FRANK:

There it is, Rita, over two thousand years of history. The Chairman stood right where you are now and he said to me, "Leeson, I'm leaving this priceless Ming vase with you because you're obviously a man of honesty and integrity, and I know our trust in you will be well placed".

RITA:

That's very nice.

FRANK:

Yes, Rita, I think before very long, I may well find myself nominated for a seat on the Club Committee.

RITA:

That really would be a feather in your cap.

FRANK:

Indeed. Meanwhile, I can enjoy the company of this magnificent vase for the next few days. Look at that craftsmanship. All hand painted. Ah, they don't have painters of that calibre today.

FADE OUT

FADE IN ON:

THE BROCKS' LIVING ROOM. EVENING.

THE ROOM IS EMPTY AS WE COME UP ON IT. FROM UPSTAIRS WE HEAR ANDY'S VOICE AS HE SINGS THE NAT KING COLE HIT SONG 'MONA LISA'. STILL SINGING, ANDY COMES DOWN THE STAIRS. WE SEE THAT HE IS NOW WEARING THE TRADITIONAL OUTFIT OF AN OLD TIME PAINTER. HE WEARS A BIG FRENCH BERET, A SMOCK, A BIG FLOPPY BOW TIE, A SALVADOR DALI MOUSTACHE, AND A GOATEE BEARD. HE IS SURPRISED THAT NO ONE IS THERE AND CALLS FOR CLAIRE.

ANDY:

(CALLS) Claire! Claire! Where are you?

CLAIRE: (VOICE OVER)

I'm in the kitchen. What do you want?

ANDY:

Come here a minute. I want you to see something.

CLAIRE COMES OUT OF THE KITCHEN WIPING HER HANDS ON A CLOTH. ANDY POSES IN HIS OUTFIT.

ANDY:

I'm ready to do the painting. What do you think?

CLAIRE:

I think you've gone mad. It's the living room being painted, not the Sistine Chapel.

ANDY:

(DISAPPOINTED) This is what all the best painters wore. I got the beret from Rubens, the smock from Monet, the moustache from Dali, and the goatee from...

CLAIRE:

Don't tell me, a goat! I can smell it from here. It's all a waste of time, Andy. I've called in a professional to do this room. We don't have it done often, but when we do I want it done properly.

ANDY:

But that's just wasting good money. Its only four simple walls. All it needs is a brush, a pot of paint and two hands.

CLAIRE:

Yes, as long as they're not your hands! I know exactly what will happen. We'll wind up with more paint on the carpet than on the walls.

ANDY:

I could put sheets down.

CLAIRE:

The way you work, Andy, we'd need more sheets than the Ku Klux Klan. I spend most of my day in this living room and I don't want it forever clogged up with sheets, ladders and paint cans.

ANDY:

I'll work quickly.

CLAIRE:

Andy, you never do anything quickly. When I asked you just to paint the upstairs window frames, you took four and a half weeks.

ANDY:

But I did a good job, didn't I?

CLAIRE:

It ought to have been good. After every brush stroke you climbed down the ladder, crossed to the other side of the road and did this.

(SHE HOLDS THUMB UP LIKE PAINTER GETTING PERSPECTIVE)

ANDY:

That's the way Kirk Douglas did it in the film 'Lust For Life'.

CLAIRE:

Well neither you nor Kirk Douglas are painting this room. I've called Mr. Elton round to give us a price. And I don't want you embarrassing me by arguing with him over money. Now, for heaven's sake, get out of that stupid costume before he arrives.

ANDY:

(FALLS DOWN ON HIS KNEES TO MAKE HIMSELF SHORTER) Couldn't I just do a Toulouse Lautrec and paint the bottom halves?

CLAIRE:

No!

ANDY:

(GETTING UP) Oh, alright.

ANDY TAKES OFF THE BERET, THE BOW TIE AND THE SMOCK. HE STARTS TO PULL OFF THE MOUSTACHE, WHICH IS STUCK ON WITH GLUE, VERY SLOWLY, FEELING THE PAIN AS EACH BIT COMES AWAY.

CLAIRE:

(IMPATIENTLY) Don't be a baby!

SHE RIPS OFF THE REMAINDER OF THE MOUSTACHE, CAUSING ANDY TO SCREAM AT THE SUDDEN PAIN. AS SOON AS HE FINISHES THAT SCREAM, SHE PULLS OFF HIS GOATEE BEARD AND HE SCREAMS IN PAIN AGAIN.

F/X: THE DOORBELL RINGS.

CLAIRE:

That'll be Mr. Elton.

ANDY:

(HOLDING HIS FACE AS IF IN PAIN) Thank Goodness.

CLAIRE:

Remember, no arguments.

CLAIRE OPENS THE DOOR AND ADMITS MR. ELTON, A PLEASANT-LOOKING LITTLE MAN IN HIS LATE SIXTIES.

CLAIRE:

Come in, Mr. Elton. This is my husband, Andy.

ANDY:

(GRUDGINGLY)   A fine painter he is, he hasn't even got a moustache!

CLAIRE:

Would you like a coffee, Mr. Elton?

ELTON:

No, thank you Mrs. Brock, I've just had a meal. And I can't stay long, I've another call to make.

CLAIRE:

Well we'll get straight down to business then, shall we? These are the walls we want painted, if we can agree on a price.

ELTON:

Oh, I'm sure we can. I'm not expensive. Being an old age pensioner I really just work for pleasure.

ANDY:

(SUDDENLY KEEN)   You don't charge money?

ELTON:

Yes. It's money that gives me the pleasure. What I meant was that I get my State Pension anyway, so I just do it for pocket money.

ANDY:

I hope you've got shallow pockets.

CLAIRE:

So how much o you think it will be Mr. Elton?

ELTON:

I can't tell you yet. I'll first have to measure the size of the area. Let me get my tape measure out.

ELTON TAKES OUT OF HIS POCKET AN EXPANDING STEEL TAPE MEASURE. HE PUTS ONE END AGAINST THE END OF THE WALLS.

ELTON:

(TO ANDY)   Would you mind holding it there for me?

ANDY HOLDS THE END OF THE TAPE MEASURE INTO THE CORNER WHERE ELTON PLACED IT.

ELTON:

(AS HE WALKS ALONG WITH THE TAPE MEASURE) Obviously the longer the wall the more it will cost.

BUSINESS HERE WHERE ANDY SWITCHES THE END OF THE TAPE MEASURE FROM HIS RIGHT HAND TO HIS LEFT HAND, THUS SHORTENING THE MEASUREMENT BY ABOUT 3 FEET.

ELTON:

(READING THE MEASUREMENT) Just fifteen feet. Hmm, I could have sworn it was about eighteen.

CLAIRE REALISES WHAT ANDY HAS DONE AND SHOUTS AT HIM FOR IT.

CLAIRE:

Andy!

ANDY:

(ALIBI-ING) Sorry, it slipped.

(HE PUTS THE END BACK IN THE CORNER)

ELTON:

(LOOKING AT TAPE MEASURE AGAIN) Yes, it is eighteen, as I thought. And the other walls look about the same. I reckon it will take me about eight hours.

ANDY:

Eight hours! For a small room like this? I could paint it in six.

CLAIRE:

Andy, you couldn't even paint a toe nail in six hours. If Mr. Elton says it takes eight hours, he should know.

ELTON:

Yes, there's a good eight hours work here. I charge $10 an hour during the week and $15 an hour on the weekend.

ANDY:

Why? Are the hours longer at weekends?

CLAIRE:

During the week would be fine for us.

ELTON:

It'll have to be a cash payment. I can't accept a cheque. If I put it through my bank account the government find out what I've earned and take it off my Pension.

CLAIRE:

Cash is alright with us.

ELTON:

Good. Then let's settle the colour you want the walls painted. Have you decided on a colour?

CLAIRE:

No, not really. What do you recommend?

ELTON:

It's up to you, really. But I could suggest yellow to match your curtains.:

CLAIRE:

What do you think Andy.

ANDY:

I think we should have red to match my bank account.

ELTON:

No, red's far too gaudy for a room like this. People often pick a colour to match something. Like one man picked a paint to match his wife's eyes.

ANDY:

That's not a bad idea. Do they make one that's short sighted?

CLAIRE:

Andy, Mr. Elton hasn't time for your silly jokes. (TO ELTON) How do you think a pale green would look in here?

ELTON:

No, not for here. Green's a bedroom colour. Restful on the eyes. It puts you to sleep. You don't want it in here.

ANDY:

No, we've got the television for that.

ELTON:

I think pink would be too feminine… grey would be too sombre… brown's too dark…

CLAIRE:

What about blue?

ELTON:

A cold colour. It's well known that seeing anything blue makes people feel cold.

ANDY:

That's not true. I saw a blue movie once and came out dripping with perspiration.

CLAIRE:

I've run out of ideas, Mr. Elton. We really should leave it to you, you're the expert.

ELTON:

If this room were mine, I'd settle for a neutral colour like cream. That goes with everything.

CLAIRE:

Yes, that sounds good. (TO ANDY) I won't ask you if you like cream, Andy, because you'll come out with some silly answer like "only with strawberries".

ANDY:

I wasn't going to say that at all. Cream's alright, as long as we have two coats.

CLAIRE:

Why two coats?

ANDY:

(SMILING) I like double cream.

CLAIRE:

Only with strawberries would have been funnier. We've agreed on the price and colour, Mr. Elton.   All that's left is the question of when you can start.

ELTON:

I can fit you in right away, if you like.

CLAIRE:

That's great. You mean you can start tomorrow morning?

ELTON:

No, tonight. Confidentially, I don't work days. Too many of them IRS snoops around trying to catch people like me earning the extra few dollars. If I work through the night, nobody knows.

CLAIRE:

That's even better. Then you won't disturb us at all.

ELTON:

I can come at eleven and be finished by seven in the morning.

CLAIRE:

Right, you can start at eleven then.

ELTON:

Ah, there is one thing I haven't mentioned. That's the paint fumes.

ANDY:

You're going to charge us for them as well!

ELTON:

The point is there's lead in paint and the fumes it gives off can be dangerous if you breathe it in while you're sleeping. So, just for the night you'll have to find somewhere else to go.

ANDY:

Ah, I thought there'd be a catch to it.

CLAIRE:

Just for one night, Andy, it's not going to hurt us to find a hotel.

ANDY:

Have you any idea what a hotel costs these days? It's more unnecessary expense.

F/X DOORBELL RINGS

ELTON:

(WORRIED) I'd better hide. It could be that nosey parker from the IRS Office.

CLAIRE HAS OPENED THE DOOR AND WE HEAR RITA'S VOICE.

RITA: (VOICE OVER - AT THE DOOR)

It's me, come to find out how you got on with the decorator.

ANDY:

(TO ELTON) You're safe - it's only the nosey parker from next door.

CLAIRE BRINGS RITA INTO THE ROOM

CLAIRE:

(TO RITA) This is Mr. Elton. (TO ELTON) Mr. Elton, my sister, Rita.

THEY AD LIB GREETINGS

CLAIRE:

The good news is that Mr. Elton can paint the room overnight.

ANDY:

The bad news is that we have to pay for a hotel.

RITA:

Why?

ANDY:

Because we'll be poisoned by the fumes and when we wake up in the morning we could be dead.

RITA:

No, I meant, why go to a hotel? We have a couch in our living room that opens up into a double bed. You're welcome to sleep at our place.

CLAIRE:

That solves our problem then. But are you sure Frank won't mind?

RITA:

I'm sure he won't. After all, what are neighbours for?

FADE OUT

FADE UP ON:

THE LEESONS' LIVING ROOM. NIGHT

OPEN ON A TWO-SHOT OF FRANK NEXT TO THE VASE ON ITS PEDESTAL.

FRANK:

(ANGRY) I don't know how you could have done this to me, Rita. Tonight of all nights, when I'm looking after the club's vase.

RITA:

In the heat of the moment I forgot about the vase. I just made the offer to be neighbourly. And after all, Claire is my sister.

FRANK:

Your sister I can take - it's that husband of hers. When the good Lord handed out brains, he was in the wrong line. Can't you be un-neighbourly and withdraw it.

RITA:

I can't cancel the invitation now. It would be embarrassing. Anyway, they'll be here any minute. I can't stop them coming.

FRANK:

I can. I'll build a moat round the house and fill it with hungry sharks.

RITA:

It's not like they're moving in for weeks. They'll only be here for one night.

FRANK:

Rita, the San Francisco earthquake was only for five minutes, and look at the damage that did! And if Andy wasn't too young, I'd swear he was responsible for that earthquake too. The man's a walking disaster.

RITA:

I'll tell him to be careful and not touch anything.

FRANK:

It won't make any difference. Not with Andy Brock. God made the world in six days. That man can destroy it in one night!

F/X: DOORBELL RINGS

RITA:

That's them.

FRANK:

Keep very quiet. Maybe if we don't answer, they'll go away.

RITA:

No Frank, I'm not doing that to my own sister. And when Andy comes in I want you to act friendly to him.

FRANK:

I don't think I can be that good an actor.

RITA:

Do it for my sake. Greet him warmly and shake his hand.

FRANK:

Alright, for your sake I'll shake Andy's hand. But I'll tell you now, I'll be wishing it was his throat.

RITA OPENS THE DOOR AND BRINGS IN ANDY & CLAIRE

CLAIRE:

Not too early, are we?

RITA:

No, just right.

CLAIRE:

(EXPLAINING) Mr. Elton's only just arrived. He took the long way getting here so he wouldn't be followed by the IRS Inspector. I think he came through Cleveland.

RITA:

I've got your bed all made up. (A WITHERING LOOK TO FRANK WHO HASN'T MOVED) Frank, say hello to Andy.

ANDY IS CARRYING A CARRIER BAG WITH HIS NIGHTCLOTHES AND TOILET THINGS IN IT. IT IS OVER HIS ARM.

FRANK:

(UNCONVINCINGLY) Nice to see you, Andy.

THEY SHAKE HANDS AND WHEN THEIR HANDS PART WE SEE THAT FRANK NOW HAS THE CARRIER BAG OVER HIS ARM. ANNOYED, HE HANDS IT BACK TO ANDY.

RITA:

If you need any extra blankets or pillows, let me know.

CLAIRE:

Please, there's no need to fuss over us. We'll be no trouble.

ANDY:

All we want is a place to put our heads.

FRANK LOOKS POINTEDLY AT A PICTURE WHICH CONTAINS A FRENCH GUILLOTINE. (EITHER A PICTURE OR ORNAMENT) THE LOOK ON HIS FACE SHOWS HE THINKS THAT WOULD BE A GOOD PLACE TO PUT ANDY'S HEAD. RITA NOTICES THIS AND STOPS IT BY SHOUTING.

RITA:

Frank! (HE REACTS TO HER CALL AND SHE HAS TO COVER UP. SHE SWITCHES TO A SWEETER TONE OF VOICE) Frank, why don't you tell Andy about some of your antiques while I show Claire the new vegetable carousel you built me in the kitchen. (LEADING CLAIRE OFF TO THE KITCHEN) You must see this, Claire, Frank is so clever with his hands...

FRANK:

I don't know whether you're really interested in art, Andy, but I have a fine collection I've built up over the years. (POINTS TO TWO PICTURES ON THE WALL) That's a Rubens... and that's a Turner... (REFERS TO SCULPTURE OF MAN AND WOMAN TOGETHER)... and that's Epstein.

ANDY:

Who's he with - Mrs. Epstein?

FRANK:

(DISGUSTED AT ANDY'S IGNORANCE) Epstein was the sculptor.

ANDY:

Oh.

FRANK:

That suit of armour (REFERS TO SUIT OF ARMOUR STANDING IN THE CORNER... it's French. Belonged to one of the Louis's

ANDY:

Joe Louis? The boxer?

FRANK:

The King Louis's. Most of the furniture in this room is French. Louis the Fourteenth sat on that chair.

ANDY:

(TOUCHES THE SEAT OF CHAIR) Still warm.

FRANK:

He and Marie Antoinette had their meals on that table… (REFERS TO LARGE TABLE IN CENTRE OF ROOM)… they had their coffee on that table (REFERS TO SMALLER COFFEE TABLE). That couch is part of the set too.

ANDY:

I can guess what they had on that.

FRANK GIVES ANDY A DIRTY LOOK, MOVES ACROSS TO ANOTHER WALL AND STANDS IN FRONT OF A TYPICAL PICASSO PAINTING. AMONG THE MANY OBJECTS IN THE PICTURE IS A SOLITARY HUMAN EYE IN THE CENTRE.

FRANK:

This is a Picasso. What an artist! Such a vivid imagination. To fully appreciate it you have to step back and study if from all angles.

ANDY STEPS BACK AND BENDS HIS HEAD THEN HIS BODY IN SEVERAL DIFFERENT CONTORTIONS TRYING TO LOOK AT THE PICTURE IN THE HOPE OF UNDERSTANDING ITS IMAGERY.

FRANK:

A picture like this one gets you here. (POINTS TO HIS OWN HEART)

ANDY:

(RUBBING HIS OWN NECK) Gets me here too.

ANDY LOOKS AWAY FROM THE PICASSO.

ANDY:

Have you run out of flowers?

FRANK:

What?

ANDY:

The vase, it's got no flowers in it.

ANDY IS ABOUT TO GO TO THE CHINESE VASE ON THE PEDESTAL. FRANK PANICS.

FRANK:

(SHOUTS) Don't go near that! (ANDY FREEZES ON THE SPOT) It's very delicate. It's Chinese.

ANDY:

Oh, I see what you mean. Claire's cousin brought one back from his holiday in Hong Kong. Very cheaply made, only lasted a fortnight.

FRANK:

That vase is over 2,000 years old! It's a Ming. But I don't suppose you've ever heard of the famous dynasty.

ANDY:

Of course I have. I watch it all the time.

FRANK:

I'm talking about the Chinese Royal Family - the Ming Dynasty. Have you any idea what that vase would cost to buy?

ANDY:

I suppose it depends

FRANK:

On what?

ANDY:

On whether you're buying it at Bloomingdale's or Woolworth's?

FRANK:

You don't buy 2,000 year old vases at Woolworths! There are only a handful of them left in the world. Can you see that inscription there on the side?

ANDY IS ABOUT TO MOVE FORWARD TO GET A CLOSER LOOK

FRANK:

Stay where you are! You can look at it from here.

ANDY CAN'T SEE IT PROPERLY FROM WHERE HE IS, SO HE TAKES HIS GLASSES OFF AND HOLDS THEM ABOUT SIX INCHES AWAY FROM HIS FACE TO USE THEM AS A MAGNIFYING GLASS. HE SQUINTS HIS EYES, BUT HE STILL CAN'T SEE THE INSCRIPTION.

FRANK:

It says…(SHORT CHINESE PHRASE)

ANDY TRIES TO REPEAT THE PHRASE AND DOES IT BADLY. FRANK COACHES HIM IN SAYING THE PHRASE WHICH ANDY REPEATS BETTER THE SECOND TIME, BUT STILL WRONG.

FRANK:

Never mind, that's near enough. It is the royal motto. It means a man without wisdom is a slave to life.

RITA AND CLAIRE COME OUT OF THE KITCHEN AT THIS POINT.

RITA:

How are you two getting on?

FRANK:

I was just showing Andy the vase and pointing out how valuable it is.

RITA:

(TO CLAIRE) Frank was telling me that it's so valuable, through the centuries men have murdered to get their hands on it.

FRANK:

(POINTEDLY - LOOKING AT ANDY) And if anyone else's hands get on it - there could be another murder tonight!

RITA:

(ANGRY AT FRANK FOR MAKING SUCH A DIRECT THREAT) Frank! (CHANGE OF TONE TO COVER UP} We really ought to let our guests go to bed, it's getting rather late.

CLAIRE:

Yes, I am feeling tired.

FRANK:

O.K. We'll go upstairs. But promise me you will be careful down here.

ANDY:

You can rely on me. I'll treat everything as if it were my own.

FRANK:

Now I'm even more worried.

RITA:

You go on ahead, Frank. I'll just lay out some clean guest towels in the bathroom and join you in a minute.

FRANK, CLAIRE AND ANDY AD LIB 'GOOD NIGHT'.
FRANK GOES UP THE STAIRS.

CLAIRE:

It's very good of Frank to let us stay the night.

RITA:

He's got a heart of gold really. It's just that sometimes he gets a bit fanatical about his valuable antiques.

CLAIRE:

You've got so many of them.

RITA:

Yes, sometimes I feel I'm not so much a housewife as a Curator of a museum.

RITA GOES INTO THE BATHROOM.

ANDY:

Do you realise that just about everything in this room is older than I am?

CLAIRE:

Yes, and from the way Frank was glaring at you, if you want to be older than you are, you had better stay away from that vase.

ANDY:

I'm not going near it. All I'm here for is to get some sleep.

CLAIRE:

Good.

RITA RETURNS FROM THE BATHROOM

RITA:

I've laid out towels and soap and a glass so you can clean your teeth. I'll just check the front door's locked and then leave you to get into your nightclothes.

RITA CHECKS THE FRONT DOOR IS PROPERLY LOCKED, THEN SHE GOES TOWARDS THE STAIRS.

RITA:

Sleep tight - see you in the morning.

THEY ALL AD LIB GOODNIGHTS - RITA GOES UP THE STAIRS.

CLAIRE:

(PICKING UP OVERNIGHT BAG) I'll clean my teeth first. You always take such a long time.

CLAIRE GOES TO THE BATHROOM.

FADE OUT

FADE UP ON:

THE LEESONS' BEDROOM: NIGHT

IT IS A WELL DECORATED ROOM, TASTEFULLY
FURNISHED. FRANK IS READING IN BED. RITA HAS GOT
INTO HER NIGHTDRESS AND IS JUST GETTING INTO BED
BESIDE FRANK.

RITA:

What are you reading?

FRANK:

Its a book on Chinese pottery. More fascinating information on that
vase downstairs.

RITA:

I'm beginning to think you care more for that damned vase than you
do for your own wife.

FRANK:

Don't be silly dear. I'll think just as much of you when you're 2,000
years old. (CLOSING THE BOOK) I'll turn the light out and read
the rest tomorrow.

HE PUTS THE BOOK ON THE BEDSIDE TABLE AND PULLS
ON THE CORD ABOVE THE BED WHICH TURNS THE
LIGHT OUT. FRANK AND RITA SETTLE DOWN TO SLEEP.

FADE OUT

FADE IN ON:

THE LEESONS' LIVING ROOM: NIGHT

CLAIRE IS ALREADY IN BED IN HER NIGHTDRESS. ANDY
IS OUT OF SIGHT IN THE BATHROOM CLEANING HIS
TEETH. HE IS GARGLING LOUDLY.

CLAIRE:

Other husbands gargle quietly. I had to marry one who thinks he's a
Swiss yodeller.

164

ANDY FINISHES CLEANING HIS TEETH AND COMES OUT
OF THE BATHROOM. HE WEARS PYJAMAS WITH A LOUD
PATTERN THAT SHOULD GET A LAUGH WHEN SEEN BY
THE AUDIENCE.

CLAIRE:

You've been twenty minutes in there. What did you do - one tooth at a
time?

ANDY:

I like to do things properly. And since we're having to put up with all
this inconvenience I hope Elton is doing a proper job next door.

CLAIRE:

He was well recommended. (REMEMBERS SOMETHING) There
was one thing I forgot to ask him.   Whether the paint was washable

ANDY:

Why? Are you going to take the walls down to the launderette?

CLAIRE:

(ANNOYED) You've got an answer for everything. As always a
stupid one. Come in to bed and turn the light out, I'm tired.

ANDY GETS INTO THE BED AND REACHES UP TO TURN
THE LIGHT OUT BUT REALISES THERE'S NO CORD (AS
FRANK HAD) NOR SWITCH ON THE WALL ABOVE THE
BED.

ANDY:

There's no light switch.

CLAIRE:

(REALISES) Oh no, of course not. It's over there by the front door.
But be careful you don't touch anything!

ANDY:

(GETTING OUT OF BED AGAIN) (SARCASTIC) Is it alright if I
touch the floor?

ANDY GOES TO THE LIGHT SWITCH NEAR THE FRONT DOOR. HE STANDS THERE LOOKING BACK AT THE ROOM.

CLAIRE:

Well! Turn the light out.

ANDY:

Don't rush me! Coming back is going to be like walking through a minefield.

HE TURNS THE LIGHT OUT. THE ROOM IS NOW ONLY LIT BY THE MOONLIGHT SHINING THROUGH THE WINDOW. ANDY SLOWLY FEELS HIS WAY PAST THE FURNITURE TOWARDS THE BED. ANDY LETS OUT A SCREAM OF PAIN AND HOLDS HIS FOOT UP AND RUBS IT.

CLAIRE:

What did you kick?

ANDY:

The leg of the table. I think I broke my toe.

CLAIRE:

That's alright then, as long as you didn't break anything important.

ANDY:

(SARCASTIC) Thanks a lot!

HE LIMPS HIS WAY BACK TO THE BED AND SITS DOWN RUBBING HIS TOE.

ANDY:

This bed feels lumpy.

CLAIRE:

That's me. Get in your own side.

ANDY:

Oh.

ANDY GETS UP AND GOES ROUND THE OTHER SIDE OF THE BED AND GETS INTO IT. HE LAYS DOWN, BUT CAN'T FIND A COMFORTABLE POSITION. HE TURNS SEVERAL TIMES.

CLAIRE:

(ANNOYED) For goodness sake, Andy, settle down.

ANDY:

I'm trying to.

CLAIRE:

You're turning so much it's like sleeping next to a cement mixer. Find yourself a position and lay still so I can get some sleep.

ANDY FINDS A POSITION.

ANDY:

Good night.

CLAIRE:

I hope so.

CAMERA PANS ACROSS TO THE FACE OF THE GRANDFATHER CLOCK AGAINST THE WALL. IT'S QUARTER PAST TWELVE.

DISSOLVE AND COME UP ON THE CLOCK NOW READING THREE O'CLOCK.

CAMERA PANS BACK FROM THE CLOCK TO ANDY IN BED, SNORING. HE SNORES TWO OR THREE TIMES THEN HIS EYES OPEN WIDE.

ANDY:

What am I snoring for - I'm not asleep. Claire… Claire… are you awake?

CLAIRE:

(HE HAS WOKEN HER UP) I am now! What do you want?

ANDY:

It's three o'clock in the morning.

CLAIRE:

You woke me to tell me that?!! I've been laying here for three hours, I can't sleep.

CLAIRE:

Count sheep jumping over a fence.

ANDY:

I did, till they stopped jumping. They fell asleep before I did. It's this bed, I'm not used to it.

CLAIRE :

So, what do you expect me to do?

ANDY:

You can do what my mother used to do when I couldn't sleep.

CLAIRE:

Forget it, you're too big now to pick up in my arms and sing a lullaby.

ANDY:

No, she used to make me a hot chocolate drink. That made me sleep like a baby.

CLAIRE:

Well do it without the hot chocolate. Stick your thumb in your mouth.

ANDY STICKS HIS THUMB IN HIS MOUTH. WE HEAR LOUD SUCKING NOISES.

ANDY:

It's not working, the noise keeps me awake.

CLAIRE:

Well stick your thumb in your ear then, but for goodness sake, let me get some sleep.

CLAIRE LAYS BACK AND FALLS ASLEEP AGAIN.

ANDY:

I'm going back next door to make myself a hot chocolate drink.

ANDY GETS OUT OF BED AND CAREFULLY PUTS HIS
SLIPPERS ON AND TIP TOES TO THE FRONT DOOR AND
OPENS IT.

ANDY:

(LOUD WHISPER - BACK TO CLAIRE) I'll leave the door
unlocked so I won't have to wake you when I come back.

CLAIRE SNORES LIGHTLY - SHE HASN'T HEARD HIM.
ANDY LEAVES THE DOOR UNLOCKED AND GOES OUT.

CUT TO:

THE BROCKS' LIVING ROOM: NIGHT

MR. ELTON IS ON A LADDER AND IS HALFWAY THROUGH
PAINTING ONE OF THE WALLS. HE HEARS THE SOUND
OF A KEY IN THE DOOR AND REACTS.

ELTON:

(ALARMED AND JUMPING TO THE WRONG CONCLUSION)

The IRS man!

IN PANIC, HE CLIMBS DOWN FROM THE LADDER WITH
HIS WIDE BRUSH STILL IN HIS HAND. HE HEARS THE
DOOR OPEN AND QUICKLY HIDES BEHIND IT, HOLDING
HIS BRUSH UP. ANDY OPENS THE DOOR WIDE AS HE
COMES IN. THE DOOR CRUSHES ELTON (BEHIND IT)
AGAINST THE WALL.

ANDY:

(LOOKS ABOUT AND DOESN'T SEE ELTON) Mr. Elton?

THE DOOR STARTS TO SWING BACK AND WE SEE ELTON
BEHIND IT WITH THE BRUSH AGAINST HIS FACE. HE
REMOVES THE BRUSH - HIS FACE IS COVERED IN PAINT.

ELTON:

It's you. What are you doing here?

ANDY:

I live here.

ELTON:

But you're supposed to be next door

ANDY:

I came back to make myself a hot chocolate. I can never sleep in a strange bed. I don't know how he does it every night.

ELTON:

Who?

ANDY:

Warren Beatty. (AN AFTERTHOUGHTJ) Well, maybe he doesn't sleep either. Would you like a hot chocolate?

ELTON:

No thanks, but I will have a cup of tea, that'll calm my nerves. You really scared me when you came through that door. At my age that can be dangerous.

BY NOW ANDY HAS GONE THROUGH TO THE KITCHEN TO MAKE THE DRINKS. ELTON SEES HIS REFLECTION IN THE WINDOW AND JUMPS BACK IN HORROR. IT'S THE PAINT ON HIS FACE THAT MAKES HIM LOOK GHOSTLIKE.

ELTON:

(REALISING THE REFLECTION WAS HIM - IS RELIEVED)

Oh, it's me.

HE SITS DOWN WITH HIS HAND AGAINST HIS PALPITATING HEART.

FADE OUT

FADE UP ON:

THE LEESONS' BEDROOM: NIGHT

THE ONLY LIGHT IS FROM THE MOONLIGHT COMING THROUGH THE WINDOW. RITA AND FRANK ARE ASLEEP IN BED. FRANK IS MUTTERING IN HIS SLEEP. HIS

MUTTERING GETS LOUDER AND MORE FRANTIC AND HE
EVENTUALLY WAKES UP SCREAMING.

FRANK:

(SCREAMING) Keep away from there! Keep away!

FRANK HAS SAT UPRIGHT AND THE SCREAMING HAS
WOKEN RITA TOO. SHE TURNS ON THE LIGHT.

FRANK:

(SWEATING) I'm sorry, dear, I was having a nightmare. It was clear
as a picture. Andy was sleep walking… and he was heading straight for
the vase.

RITA:

Do you know what I think, Frank? I think the best thing would be for
you to bring the vase up here tonight so you'll know it's safe.

FRANK:

(LIKES THE IDEA) Of course! I don't know why I didn't think of
that in the first place. I'll do it now.

RITA:

But do it quietly. We don't want to wake our guests.

FRANK PUTS HIS SLIPPERS ON AND HEADS FOR THE
DOOR.

CUT TO:

THE LEESONS' LIVING ROOM: NIGHT

BY THE LIGHT OF THE MOON, WE SEE FRANK QUIETLY
CREEPING DOWN THE STAIRS. HE STOPS AT THE
BOTTOM OF THE STAIRS AND LISTENS TO MAKE SURE HE
HASN'T WOKEN ANYONE UP. THEN HE CROSSES TO THE
VASE, CAREFULLY LIFTS IT OFF THE PEDESTAL AND TIP
TOES BACK TO THE STAIRS WITH IT. HE ONCE AGAIN
CHECKS TO SEE HE HASN'T WOKEN ANYONE, THEN
GOES BACK UPSTAIRS.

CAMERA PANS ACROSS THE ROOM FOR A CLOSE UP OF CLAIRE ASLEEP.

FADE OUT

FADE UP ON:

THE BROCKS' LIVING ROOM. NIGHT

MR. ELTON IS BACK UP ON THE LADDER PAINTING THE WALL. ANDY IS JUST FINISHING DRINKING HIS MUG OF HOT CHOCOLATE.

ANDY:

That's better, I feel more relaxed now.

ELTON:

You think you'll be able to sleep?

ANDY :

I ought to. I put a sleeping pill in the drink for good measure. I ought to be able to sleep like Rip Van Winkle.

ELTON:

I hope not. I'm an old man - I can't wait that long to get paid.

ANDY SEES THAT ELTON HAS HARDLY SIPPED HIS CUP OF TEA.

ANDY:

Don't forget your tea, it's getting cold.

ELTON:

Yes, I'll drink it in a minute. I just want to finish this corner first.

ANDY:

O.K. I'll see you in the morning.

ANDY GOES. WE STAY WITH ELTON PAINTING. ANDY HAD LEFT HIS MUG NEXT TO THE PAINT POT. ELTON DIPS HIS BRUSH IN THE MUG AND PAINTS A CHOCOLATE STREAK.

CUT TO:

THE LEESONS' LIVING ROOM: NIGHT

THERE IS JUST THE MOONLIGHT THROUGH THE
WINDOW AS THE DOOR OPENS AND ANDY COMES IN.

ANDY:

(LOUD WHISPER TO CLAIRE) Claire I'm back. (THERE'S NO
REPLY) She's still asleep, I'd better not turn the light on.

ANDY TRIES TO FIND HIS WAY BACK TO THE BED IN THE
DARK AND BUMPS INTO THE PEDESTAL. HE SCREAMS. IT
WAKES CLAIRE UP.

CLAIRE:

(WAKING UP WITH A START) What happened?

ANDY:

I bumped into the pedestal.

CLAIRE:

Oh no! You haven't hurt the vase? Turn on the light.

ANDY TURNS THE LIGHT ON. HE SEES THE VASE IS NOT
ON THE PEDESTAL AND LOOKS FOR IT ON THE FLOOR.

ANDY:

It's not here!

CLAIRE:

It's got to be there!

ANDY:

It was on the pedestal when I went out. Maybe I knocked it then. I'll
retrace my footsteps.

ANDY DOES BUSINESS OF WALKING BACKWARDS TO THE
BED LIKE A FILM BEING REVERSED, BUMPING INTO A
COUPLE OF THINGS ON THE WAY (MAYBE THE SUIT OF
ARMOUR TO WHICH HE SAYS "Sorry"). CLAIRE HAS NOW

GOT OUT OF BED AND IS LOOKING ON THE FLOOR FOR THE VASE.

CLAIRE:

Where can it be? Vases don't have legs, they can't just walk away. And you locked the door when you went out, didn't you?

ANDY:

(GUILTY) Did I...?

CLAIRE:

(HORRIFIED) Andy, you didn't just walk out of the house with that vase there and leave the door unlocked?

ANDY:

(GUILTY) Didn't I...?

CLAIRE:

How could you do such a stupid thing? You've let a burglar walk in and steal a 2,000 year old priceless Ming vase. Frank will go mad.

ANDY:

Don't panic. Just let me think this through quietly and calmly. (PAUSE) Alright, I've thought it through.

CLAIRE:

Now what do we do?

ANDY:

Let's panic.

CLAIRE:

That vase isn't even Frank's. He'll be in real trouble.

ANDY:

(HAS AN IDEA) I've got the answer. We'll replace it so no-one'll know it's gone.

CLAIRE:

(SARCASTIC) And just where do you think we're going to get a 2,000 year old vase this time of night?

ANDY:

I don't know, ask the burglar - he got one.

CLAIRE:

This is a fine way to repay Frank for his hospitality. I just don't know what we're going to tell him in the morning.

ANDY:

It was my fault Claire. So when he comes down here in the morning, I'll tell the truth. After all, honesty is the best policy.

CLAIRE:

He'll kill you.

ANDY:

(BACKING DOWN) Maybe I should settle for second best. I should never have left the house

CLAIRE:

Right.

ANDY:

I'd have done better to have left the country.

CLAIRE:

Maybe I'm imagining all this. Perhaps I'll wake up in the morning and find this was just a dream. (CHANGES HER MIND) No, it couldn't be. It's always Paul Newman in my dreams, not you.

ANDY:

(FACE LIGHTS UP) Hey, I've had a thought.

CLAIRE:

(SARCASTICALLY) Well sit down and rest for a minute - it'll go away.

ANDY:

Insurance. A valuable thing like that must have been insured against theft.

CLAIRE:

It probably was, but that doesn't help. The insurance company would want proof of a break-in. And there wasn't any. Can you imagine telling them that the man left in charge of that vase was stupid enough to leave the door open so a thief could just walk in?

ANDY:

They'd never believe it!

CLAIRE:

They would if they saw you; but that doesn't get Frank off the hook with his club. There's no sign of a burglary, no proof the vase was taken. They could even accuse Frank of stealing the vase himself.

ANDY:

I hadn't thought of that. They could throw him out of the Club.

CLAIRE:

Yes, out of the Club and straight into jail. And all because of you. I just wish there was something we could do to help.

ANDY:

I've had another thought.

CLAIRE:

Andy Brock, I don't know what silly scheme is lurking in what passes for that brain of yours, but forget it. You've done enough damage for one night.

ANDY:

But this idea will not only get Frank out of trouble, he'll thank me for helping him. What I need is that plaster out of the First Aid Box in the bathroom.

HE GOES TOWARDS THE BATHROOM.

CLAIRE:

Andy, what are you going to do?

ANDY:

You'll see. And you're going to be proud of me.

ANDY GOES TO BATHROOM. CLOSE IN ON CLAIRE'S
WORRIED LOOK.
FADE OUT

FADE UP ON:

THE LEESONS' BEDROOM: NIGHT

FRANK AND RITA ARE BOTH SLEEPING PEACEFULLY.
FRANK TURNS OVER IN HIS SLEEP HIS ARM DROPS OVER
THE SIDE OF THE BED.

CAMERA PANS DOWN HIS ARM AND WE SEE THE VASE IS
HIDDEN UNDER THE BED.

FRANK SNORES LIGHTLY.

FADE OUT

FADE UP ON:

THE LEESONS' LIVING ROOM: EARLY MORNING

CAMERA SLOWLY PANS ROUND THE ROOM WHICH NOW
LOOKS AS IF IT HAS BEEN HIT BY A TORNADO.   CHAIRS
ARE OVERTURNED, BOOKS AND ORNAMENTS HAVE
FALLEN OFF THE SHELVES ONTO THE FLOOR.   THE
PAINTINGS ON THE WALL ARE HANGING AT ODD
ANGLES, THE PLUSH CURTAINS ARE HALF PULLED DOWN.

CLAIRE: (VOICE OVER)

I'll say this for you Andy, you're no good at making things, but you're
great at breaking them.

WE HEAR A RIPPING OF PLASTER AND CUT TO ANDY AT
THE WINDOW.   HE HAS STUCK A RING OF PLASTER ON
THE LOWER HALF OF THE WINDOW.

ANDY:

Yes, it was quite a fight I put up. And here's where the burglar got in.
I saw this on an episode of *Kojak*.

ANDY PICKS UP HIS SHOE AND TAPS THE WINDOW IN THE AREA COVERED BY THE PLASTER. THE WINDOW BREAKS WITH VERY LITTLE NOISE.

ANDY:

(EXPLAINING TO CLAIRE) The plaster stops the noise so it doesn't wake them upstairs. Brilliant, eh?

CLAIRE:

(SARCASTIC) Very, especially as the plaster is on this side, so he had to get in first before he could break in.

ANDY:

(REALISES SHE'S RIGHT) Oh, well I've got time. You take the plaster off this side while I go out and put some on the other side.

ANDY GOES TO THE DOOR AND GOES OUT, RETURNS IMMEDIATELY AND PUTS BOLT OF LOCK DOWN SO THAT WHEN HE GOES OUT AGAIN IT LOCKS.

CLAIRE:

Now he locks the door!

ANDY TURNS UP ON OTHER SIDE OF THE WINDOW AND STARTS PUTTING THE PLASTER ON.

FADE OUT

FADE UP ON:

THE LEESONS' BEDROOM: MORNING
CAMERA PULLS OUT FROM THE RINGING ALARM CLOCK THAT SHOWS IT IS EIGHT O'CLOCK. RITA PUSHES THE BUTTON THAT TURNS OFF THE ALARM.

FRANK:

Is it eight o'clock already?

RITA:

Yes. Time to get up and make our guests some breakfast.

FRANK:

I must say it was a much more restful night than I expected, thanks to the vase being up here.

RITA:

You see, it costs very little to be neighbourly after all. I'll put the kettle on, you come down as soon as you're ready.

BY NOW RITA IS OUT OF BED AND IS PUTTING HER DRESSING GOWN ON.

CUT TO:

THE LEESONS' LIVING ROOM: MORNING

ANDY BY NOW HAS THE TOP OF HIS PYJAMAS TORN.

ANDY:

Here they come. I hope this works. I'm doing it for Frank.

CLAIRE:

I hope it works too. I'll tell you one thing, you're not as good a lover as Paul Newman, but you'll have to be a better actor.

WE HEAR THE DOOR OPEN AND CLOSE UPSTAIRS.

ANDY GETS HIMSELF INTO A POSE OF AN EXHAUSTED, ALMOST CRIPPLED FIGHTER.

RITA:

(COMING DOWN THE STAIRS) Good morning! I hope you two had a peaceful… (SHE SEES THE DEVASTATION) My God, what happened?

THIS IS ANDY'S TOUR DE FORCE BIT OF BUSINESS WHERE HE THROWS HIMSELF AROUND THE ROOM DEMONSTRATING THE FIGHT THAT WAS SUPPOSED TO HAVE TAKEN PLACE.

ANDY:

(HAM ACTING) It was terrible, Rita. This big burglar, six foot twelve about 250 pounds in his socks. He came through the window…I saw him and I got out of bed and I said, 'You're not stealing anything from my best friend, Frank.' And he hit me against the wall… but I came back and I said, 'I'm not letting you get away with any of my best friend Frank's antiques.' And he punched me across here… and when I got up, he punched me across there… But I refused to give in. I told him 'You can do your worst, but I'll fight to the death for my best friend Frank.'

DURING THIS LAST SENTENCE CLAIRE HAS SEEN FRANK COMING DOWN THE STAIRS HOLDING THE VASE.

CLAIRE:

Andy, don't look now, but I think you just lost your best friend!

THEY ALL LOOK UP AT FRANK ON THE STAIRS AS HE SURVEYS THE STATE OF THE ROOM AND BREAKS INTO TEARS.

FRANK:

And I thought I was joking when I said he caused the San Francisco earthquake.

FADE OUT

FADE UP ON:

THE BROCKS' LIVING ROOM: DAY

THE ROOM APPEARS TO HAVE NOBODY IN IT. THE STATE OF THE DECORATION IS MORE OR LESS THE SAME AS WHEN ANDY LEFT ELTON EARLIER. THERE IS NO SIGN OF ELTON AT THE MOMENT.

THE DOOR OPENS AND ANDY AND CLAIRE ENTER IN THEIR NORMAL CLOTHES. ANDY CARRIES AN OVERNIGHT BAG.

THEY TALK AS THEY ENTER.

CLAIRE:

I think Frank acted very calmly under the circumstances.

ANDY :

Yes, he didn't show his temper at all till the last minute when I offered to repair the window.

CLAIRE:

(LOOKS AROUND)

Hey, the room, it's not finished.

ANDY:

It's just the same as when I left it.

CLAIRE:

(CALLING) Mr. Elton, Mr. Elton!

ANDY:

Maybe he's in the kitchen.

ANDY GOES TO THE KITCHEN.

ANDY: (VOICE OVER FROM KITCHEN)

I've found him.

ANDY COMES FROM THE KITCHEN WITH ELTON IN HIS ARMS UNCONSCIOUS

CLAIRE:

What happened? Is he alright?

ANDY:

Yes, he's just asleep. (HE DROPS ELTON ONTO THE COUCH. IT WAKES HIM UP)

ELTON:

(WAKING UP STARTLED) What happened?

CLAIRE:

You tell us.

ELTON:

I just drank the tea Mr. Brock left me… and that's all I remember.

CLAIRE:

(ACCUSINGLY AT ANDY) Andy!

ANDY:

Well, anybody could accidentally put a sleeping pill in the wrong cup...

CLAIRE:

No, only you could.

ELTON:

I'll come back and finish it tonight. But you'll have to find somewhere to stay again.

CLAIRE:

We can't ask them again next door.

ANDY:

We don't have to. I've got a better idea.

FADE OUT

FADE UP ON:

THE BROCKS' BACK GARDEN: NIGHT

CAMERA STAYS OUTSIDE THE MISSHAPEN SHED THAT ANDY BUILT. WE HEAR THE VOICES OF ANDY AND CLAIRE WHO ARE INSIDE THE SHED.

CLAIRE:

Goodnight, Andy.

ANDY:

Goodnight, Claire.

CLAIRE:

Close the door.

WE SEE THE DOOR - WHICH IS STILL IN THE ROOF OF THE SHED - BEING SLAMMED SHUT.

ROLL CLOSING CREDITS.

LESSON NINE: Finding Markets For Your Work.

Having written your masterpiece, your next step is to find a market so you can profit from your hard work. Obviously the largest paycheck will come from writing episodes of sitcoms for which you should get anything from £5,000 to £10,000 depending on the time slot and how many repeats there are. Royalties can go on for years. Satellite TV stations are still repeating many series from up to forty years ago. They don't often repeat shows broadcast prior to 1966, because that's when colour TV started in the U.K. Though there were only twelve episodes of *Fawlty Towers*, John Cleese and Connie Booth are still raking in the royalties today. Not just from the airing on TV, but from the commercial videos that have sold in the millions.

Let us suppose that, like this course in comedy writing, you have started with just writing gags and routines. How do you sell them? Currently on television and radio there are a raft of comedy panel shows featuring comedians. The producers of these shows usually have a budget to buy topical gags that can be inserted into their shows as supposed ad-libs by either members of the panel or the host. You don't always get the glory of a credit, but you will get paid. I don't know what the current fee is, but in the days of BBC Radio's *News Huddlines* and *Week Ending* non-contracted writers got £13 a gag which, with a repeat later the same week came to about £20.

Payment for writing for comedians performing in theatres, nightclubs or on cruises is negotiable. Some only pay £5 a gag while others pay up to £20.

For instance, Bob Monkhouse was earning £10,000 a show and was determined to change his material as often as possible to keep his act fresh. I was just one of four writers Bob kept on the £8,000 retainer. Of course one has to build up a relationship with a comedian by first sending them the right gags that will fit their style of performing. The initial first few batches will submitted on spec.

How do you make contact with comedians in the first place? Through a company called AVALON, which you can call up via Google on the internet, you can get a weekly listing of the dates and venues dozens of top solo comedians are working. You can send samples of your best gags to those comedians at those venues. Or; if a particular venue is near where you live, pop along and meet the performer in person.

If the comedians you choose are appearing in a TV or radio show, write to the BBC or ITV Ticket Office who will supply you with tickets (free of charge) to attend the show. This gives you the opportunity to approach the comedian in person after the show. It is no use you creating the greatest gags of all time if no one knows about them. Till you have built up a reputation for consistent, high quality gags you have to do your own hawking them around.

The internet has made the job a lot easier than when I started out as a gag writer. Now you can email your topical gags to producers in the UK and abroad in a matter of seconds without worrying about postal delays. Comedian Rudi Carrell hosted a topical comedy show in Bremen in Germany for six months. Every Tuesday evening he emailed me with whatever events were in the news that week. I had till Thursday lunchtime to come up with gags on those subject and email them back to him. He paid £30 for every gag he used on the show. So you are not just restricted to selling your gags here in Britain.

Sketch shows are not as prevalent now as they were in the past. The Russ Abbot, Hale & Pace, Smith & Jones, Little & Large, Dave Allen and Jasper Carrott shows of that type are gone. However, there are plans in the pipeline for more sketch shows on TV and BBC Radio. Watch out for the advance publicity and send your sample sketches in as soon as possible. The BBC very obligingly have their *Writers Room* on the internet which will not only keep you informed of current and future show, but have a vast library of already-produced scripts you can download and study free of charge. Call up *The Writers Room* on line and register your name with them to receive a regular newsletter.

If you've written a routine that you haven't been able to sell, then consider adapting it as a magazine article. Most magazine editors love to publish articles that show the funny side of a subject their readers might like. So, when you have finished writing the piece, go along to the Reference Section of your local library and look through their copy of either *Benn's Press Directory* or *Willings Press Guide*. There you will find a comprehensive list of newspapers and magazines covering just about every subject you could ever think of. Pick one that covers the subject you've satirized and send it to the named editor and address of that magazine. Payments vary according to the size of the magazine's circulation, so start by selecting one that shows it has the largest circulation. Address it to the Editor or Features Editor by their name rather than their position.

When you have had your grounding in those fields you'll probably be itching to join the big boys writing sitcoms. Because of the large rewards, this can be a very competitive field. When my friend Vernon Lawrence was Head Of Comedy at ITV he said he received, on average, about 1,000 ideas for sitcoms from new writers. Of those, again on average, he selected just 34 as being worth serious consideration. After discussion with his executive colleagues they were whittled down to eight to be tried out as pilot shows. Half of those proved promising enough to be made into series. I should point out that probably 70% of those 1,000 were just submitted as ideas, rather than completed scripts and were rejected for that very reason Unless you are an established writer with a proven record, you have very little chance of selling just an idea for a sitcom. It has to be a full script.

These days submitted scripts are read by Commissioning Editors who either reject them or pass them up them up to their superiors with a letter of recommendation. It usually takes about four months before a new writer whose script has been chosen to actually be called in to do re-writes or go ahead with a series. The reasons for this are many. It could be the star they have in mind for the lead is not currently available, or they are trying out another new sitcom that may clash, or they have enough shows in the pipeline waited to be piloted and don't have the budget at this moment for another. It even could be that they have enough scripts in the waiting from top writers they don't want to take the risk of commissioning someone new who might not be able to keep the standard up for a whole series.

All these things can put a new writer off, but new writers are breaking in all the time. Mainly because they are persistent. If one company turned their script down they offered it to another. There's a long history of shows whose potential was overlooked by one company and proved a huge success by their rival.

If you have written a sitcom script my advice to you is to try to avoid it joining the bottom of the pile of to-be-read scripts by a Commissioning Editor. A good short cut is to send it to whichever well known actor or actress you think would be ideal. If they like it then their agent will push it through to the top TV executives. Check via *The Stage* newspaper whether that actor/actress is currently appearing in a theatre and, if they are, send your script to them there. Or you can send it to their agent whose name and address you can find in a cheap-to-buy booklet entitled *Artists And Their Agents*. As an added incentive you can tell the agent that you are unrepresented and you will be pleased to have them handle your contract if the script is accepted.

Remember, this can apply to radio as well as television. Some star names are too busy with their stage and film work to take weeks off for the rehearsals and recording of a TV series. On radio they just have to read a scripts into the microphone after a short rehearsal so each show shouldn't take up more than half a day of their time.

I'm sure the thought running through your mind is why go to all the bother of trying to market your material when there are dozens of good literary agents who specialize in that job. The problem is that most of them have their client list already full. But as writers get old and either die or retire, they will want to fill those gaps. Here's a list of reliable literary agents you might want to approach with your written work to see if they are interested in representing you.

BLAKE FRIEDMANN Literary, TV and Film Agency

122 Arlington Road, London NW1 7HP.

Tel: 020 7284 0408   www.blakefriedmann.co.uk

CURTIS BROWN GROUP LTD.

5TH. Floor, Haymarket House, 28-29 Haymarket, London SW1 4SP

Tel: 020 73934400   www.curtisbrown.co.uk

JFL Agency, 48 Charlotte St, London W1T 2NS

Tel: 020 3137 8182   www.jflagency.com

(Initial contact by letter / email before submitting material)

ERIC GLASS LTD

25, Ladbroke Crescent, Notting Hill, London W11 1PS

Tel: 020 7229 9500

LINDA SEIFERT MANAGEMENT

4th Floor, 104 Great Portland Street, London W1W 6PE.

Tel: 020 7636 9154   www.lindaseifert.com

CECILY WARE LITERARY AGENTS

19c, John Spencer Square, London N1 2LZ

Tel: 020 7359 3787   www.cecilyware.com

        I would stress that though being on a top agent's client list does establish you as a writer of merit, it is not a necessity to have an agent at all. For the past thirty years of my career I have done my own selling and found dozens of lucrative markets abroad that British literary agents often ignore.

It was way back in 1963 I discovered the need for good comedy scripts in The Netherlands and wrote over three hundred shows for them. Then in 1971 I began writing for German TV Companies who needed material for all their top TV comedy stars. For four years I was Comedy Consultant on *Samstag Nacht*, their weekly Saturday night satire show. After that came commissioned work for TV Companies in Austria, Belgium, Norway, Denmark, Sweden, Finland, Switzerland, Canada and America. Going global provided me with an ever expanding market. A fantastic market for you too, if you if you can sustain a high enough standard of material.

Language is no problem. I write and speak only in English. My scripts are translated in-house by the foreign TV companies themselves. I just have to ensure that the humour I supply them with does not get lost in the translation. My comedy has to be universal.

Obviously you do not know what scripts are needed and by which TV companies. You have to find out by sending a few examples of your best work to their Head of Light Entertainment with an accompanying letter which says something along the lines of "Here are some samples of the kind of comedy I specialize in writing. Please let me have details of the shows you are currently producing, or have plans to produce in the near future, and I will be happy to supply scripts (gags, routine, sketches, sitcom episodes) for them."

Here is a list of some of the TV Production Companies I've dealt with. I suggest you choose one from each country to start with and begin to build your worldwide market.

AUSTRIA.

OSTERRIESCHER RUNDFUNK, Wurzburggasse 30, 1136 Wien, Austria.

BELGIUM

D&D PRODUCTIONS, Ransbeekstraat 230, B 1120 Brussels, Belgium.

CANADA

SALTER STREET FILMS, 1668 Barrington Street, Suite 500, B3J 2A2 Halifax, Nova Scotia, Canada/

CBC BROADCASTING CORPORATION, 205 Wellington Street West, PO Box 500, Station A, Toronto, Ontario M5W 1E 6, Canada.

CTV INC., 9 Channel Nine Court, Toronto M1S 4B 5, Canada

DENMARK

DANMARKS RADIO (DR TV), Rugaardsvej 25, 5100 Odense, Denmark.

DANMARKS RADIO (DR TV), TV-Byen, 2860 Soborg, Denmark.

MASTIFF A/S (previously WEGELIUS TV), Vermundsgade 40D, DK 2100, Copenhagen, Denmark

FINLAND

Oy FILMITEOLLISUUS FINE Ab, Vanha Talvitie 11a, Helsinki 00580, Finland.

Broadcasters Oy, Kajaaninkatu 6, 00510 Helsinki, Finland

MTV Oy, Ilmalantori 2, 00240 Helsinki, Finland

YLE-FINNISH BROADCASTING COMPANY, Radiokatu 5, 00024 Yleisradio, Helsinki, Finland.

GERMANY

PROSIEBEN TELEVISION, Medienallee 7, 85773 Unterfohring, Grermany.

WESTDEUTSCHER RUNDFUNK, Appellhofplatz 1, 50667 Koln, Germany.

ENTERTAINMENT FACTORY, Kirchplatz 1, 82049 Pullach, Isartal, Germany.

DIBS FILM, Kolner Strasse 43, 42781 Haan, Germany.

BRAINPOOL TV GmbH., Schanzenstrasse 22, 51063 Koln, Germany.

RTL TELEVISION GMBH., Aachener Strasse 1044, 50858 Koln, Germany.

SAT. 1 FERNSEHEN GMBH., Oberwallstrasse 6, 10117 Berlin, Germany.

G.A.T.   Infanteriestrasse 19, Haus 2, 80797 Munchen, Germany.

BR-BAYERISCHER RUNDFUNK, FS Unterhaltung, Rivastrasse 1, 85774, Unterfohring, Germany.

ITALY

RAI RADIOTELEVISIONE ITALIANA, Viale Mazzini 14, 00195 Roma, Italy.

NETHERLANDS

TROS TV, PO Box 28450, 1202 LL Hilversum, Netherlands.

NCRV TV, 'S-Gravelandseweg 80, 1217 EW Hilversum, Netherlands

NORWAY

NRK, NRK-TV, FUHA/FG41, 0340 Oslo, Norway.

SWEDEN

SVT-SVERIGES TELEVISION, Oxenstiernsgatan 26-34, 105 10 Stockholm,Sweden

SOUTH AFRICA

PENGUIN FILMS, PO Box 21716, Kloof Street, Tamboerskloof, 8001 Cape Town, South Africa.

SPAIN

EL TERRAT DE PRODUCCIONS S.L., Denia 1-3 bahos, 08006 Barcelona, Spain.

EUROPRODUCCIONES TV, C/Virgilio 5, Pozuelo de Alarcon, 28223 Madrid, Spain.

PRIME TIME COMMUNICATIONS, Pza Pablo Ruiz Picasso, Torre Picasso Tower Pd 42, 28020 Madrid, Spain.

SWITZERLAND

SRF (formerly SF-DRS-SWISS TELEVISION), Fernsehstrasse 1-4, 8052 Zurich, Switzerland.

I have deliberately omitted the contact phone numbers or email addresses because some of them may have changed by the time you read this. But you'll find them all listed on the internet, via Google, with their current details. If you want to take the trouble to phone them the operator will give you the name of their current Head of Light Entertainment so you can address him by name.

I wish you the best of luck with your endeavours and look forward to spotting your name in future TV and radio credits!

INDEX OF NAMES